Essays in Modern History (1914-89)

25 key questions answered

Russel Tarr

Edited by Andy Dailey

ACTIVEHISTORY BOOKS

books.activehistory.co.uk

First published 2020
Typeset in Palatino Linotype

Published by ActiveHistory Books
books.activehistory.co.uk

ISBN: 9781838181406

Photographic acknowledgements
Cover image: painting of Berlin Dom by the author (1994). All other images are provided for educational and illustrative purposes and are believed to be in the public domain; every reasonable effort has been made to confirm this fact through reverse image searching.

DEDICATION

To all my students, past and present, who have made history teaching so enjoyable over the years.

CONTENTS

FOREWORD

I first met Russel Tarr in Athens, Greece in Summer 2005 when I was giving my first History workshop for the International Baccalaureate. It was the hottest summer in my memory as the building had no air-conditioning and had the decor of a nuclear bomb shelter. Despite this, Russel and I enjoyed discussing a wide range of historical and professional issues over several days. Since then we have remained in close contact as historians, colleagues, and friends. Russel is an exceptional educator and historian who is held in high regard in the international teaching community.

His *Essays in Modern History* is a much needed and very welcome work. As historians and students of history, we usually have one or two areas of expertise through our studies. Most of us have studied one or two periods of time or major historical events in our studies. However, Russel's interests, studies, and teaching covers the entire 20th century with special attention to the causes and consequences of World War One, the Spanish Civil War and the Korean War; the rise of dictators such as Stalin, Franco and Castro; the rule of Lenin, Mao and Pinochet; the foreign policies of Hitler and Mussolini; Cold War crises and conflicts in Germany and Vietnam; and the success of various post-war US Presidents. This depth and breadth of knowledge is exceptional and assures us that this work on twentieth-century history is not limited in terms of scope.

By reading the twentieth-century essays presented here, one can appreciate the thorough research that has been invested in addressing the questions. Written in accessible prose, Russel's exemplar essays display a masterful use of quotes and weighing of evidence with discerning analysis. Editing this work was a pleasure; it is an excellent book which every teacher and student of modern history will find invaluable.

Andy Dailey
El Fashn, Egypt, August 2020

INTRODUCTION

Since beginning my career as a history teacher in the 1990s I have made a regular habit of writing essays along with my students – sometimes in timed examination conditions, and sometimes as more extended pieces for publication in magazines such as *History Review*. As well as helping to consolidate my own essential knowledge of each topic, these have served to provide useful discussion points during classroom feedback sessions and as revision material in the examination season.

What follows is a collection of those essays answering some of the most engaging questions covering the period 1917-1989 which have frequently appeared in examination papers. It is hoped that they will provide teachers and students not only with some helpful pointers in terms of the main perspectives on interesting topics in modern history, but also some indications about the stylistic demands of essay-writing.

Russel Tarr
Toulouse, France, August 2020

The Russian Provisional Government of 1917, including Milyukov (top left), Prince Lvov (top centre) and Kerensky (top right).

1. WAS THE 1917 BOLSHEVIK REVOLUTION A POPULAR UPRISING OR A COUP D'ETAT?

In February 1917, after three disastrous years embroiled in World War One, Tsar Nicholas II abdicated and power was handed to a Provisional Government broadly committed to a liberal democratic programme. The reasons behind the subsequent overthrow of this government and its replacement with a Bolshevik dictatorship in 1917 have been fiercely debated ever since. Sheila Fitzpatrick contends that the Provisional Government had lost all credibility by October 1917, when Lenin was swept to power on a wave of popular support. In contrast, Richard Pipes argues that the Provisional Government was still broadly popular, and that Lenin seized power in a brutal coup d'état in direct opposition to the broad wishes and interests of the Russian people. The truth is somewhere in the middle. Fitzpatrick is right that the Provisional Government was deeply unpopular by the time of its overthrow, but at the same time Pipes is correct to assert that there was no popular clamour for a Bolshevik alternative.

In political terms, the Provisional Government lacked both authority and power. Its authority was undermined by the fact that it was an unelected body, consisting broadly of moderate liberals, headed by the aristocratic Prince Lvov. Directly after the abdication of the Tsar, the Petrograd Soviet (the workers' council which controlled the factories and which was therefore essential for the war effort) issued "Order Number One". This commanded all Russian soldiers and sailors to obey their officers and the new government only if their instructions did not contradict the decrees of the Petrograd Soviet. At a stroke, this severely curtailed the Provisional Government and created what Lenin called "Dual Power", summarized by the historian Steve Smith as "An institutional arrangement under which the Provisional Government enjoyed formal authority, but where the Soviet Executive Committee had real power". The appointment into the government of Alexander Kerensky, a member of the Petrograd Soviet and a Social Revolutionary, helped superficially to maintain a degree of cooperation between the government and the Petrograd Soviet, but this relationship was to grow increasingly strained in the months ahead. Guchkov, the first Minister of War in the new government, complained to General Alexseev that "One can assert bluntly that the Provisional Government exists only as long as it is permitted to do so by the Soviet … In particular, in the military department, it is possible at present to issue only such orders as basically do not contradict [its] decisions".

However, militarily speaking, it was the Milyukov Telegram and the Kerensky Offensive which fatally undermined the credibility of the Provisional Government much more than Order Number One. The decision of the new government to continue fighting the war was not, in itself, unpopular; rather, it had been the inept handling of the war and the recklessness with which the Tsarist regime had squandered lives that had rankled so deeply. However, any hope that the new government would conduct the war any better quickly evaporated. Firstly, in April

1917 foreign minister Paul Milyukov was forced to resign when it became known that he had secretly reassured Russia's foreign allies that the new government remained committed to the Tsar's ambitious, annexationist war objectives. This directly contradicted the government's official "Declaration of War Aims" issued shortly beforehand, which had committed Russia to a "peace without annexations or indemnities", severely undermining the credibility of the new regime. Secondly, at the start of July 1917 the new minister of war, Alexander Kerensky, launched another offensive designed to restore morale but which instead ended in another 400,000 casualties and a retreat of 150 miles by the end of the month.

Its decision to continue fighting the war meant that the Provisional Government was unable to improve the social conditions of the proletariat and the peasantry. Along with its grand "Declaration of War Aims", the Provisional Government issued its "Eight Principles" which, among other things, promised an amnesty for political prisoners, freedom of speech and press and a democratically elected constituent assembly. However, the demands of the proletariat for an eight-hour working day and of the peasantry for thorough land reform were not addressed. Whilst the Provisional Government claimed that these issues would be addressed by the election of the Constituent Assembly, this was cold comfort given the fact that these elections would not be able to take place until if and when the war was fought to a successful conclusion; this appeared increasingly unlikely as time wore on. In April 1917 the Petrograd metal workers stated that "The government cannot and does not want to represent the wishes of the toiling people, and so we demand its immediate abolition and arrest of its members". Kerensky hardly succeeded in dispelling this impression when, after becoming Prime Minister in July, he promptly moved into the Tsar's private apartments. This led the

Bolshevik leader Leon Trotsky to accuse him, not unreasonably, as having "Bonapartist tendencies".

It is therefore clear that the Provisional Government was beset with all manner of political, military and social troubles by the time of its overthrow in October 1917. However, it would be a mistake to extrapolate from this that there must have been a corresponding growth of support for the Bolsheviks. Instead, the picture that emerges is of Lenin selectively building up a concentrated base of social, political and military power and then cynically using this revolutionary vanguard to smuggle himself into power under the pretence of representing the will of the people.

Socially, Lenin vigorously used propaganda in an attempt to legitimize his bid for power, but never won mass support among the peasantry or even among the proletariat which he claimed to represent. His talent for sloganeering ("Peace, Bread, Land!"), pamphleteering (the "April Theses") and scholarly persuasion ("State and Revolution") was unparalleled. He cleverly appealed to the war weariness of the average soldier ("Peace"), to the proletariat's desire for food ("Bread") and the peasantry's desire for property ("Land"). By October, a majority of members in the Petrograd Soviet were card-carrying Bolsheviks and their support was crucial in the revolution that followed. Nevertheless, Trotsky's claim that "What is taking place is not a conspiracy but an insurrection…the masses gathered under our banner" was overstating the case, to put it mildly. Growing Soviet membership does not correspond to a growth of Bolshevik support. At the first All-Russian Congress of Soviets at the beginning of June 1917, 285 Soviets were controlled by the Social Revolutionaries, 248 by the Mensheviks, 105 by the Bolsheviks and 32 by the Menshevik Internationalists.

Politically, the Bolsheviks increased their popularity to a degree during 1917, but didn't even pretend to desire a broad political coalition against the Provisional Government. This, of course, is not surprising, since a fundamental guiding principle of the Bolsheviks was their contempt for uncoordinated mass movements. Rather, they believed that only a cadre of professional revolutionaries could succeed in achieving a Marxist revolution (it was primarily on this issue that they had split away from their fellow communists, the Mensheviks, in 1903). True, in June 1917 the Bolshevik party had 24,000 members; by September this had reached 200,000. Nevertheless, this still contrasts with the 1 million members of the Social Revolutionaries, the party which represented the peasantry (roughly 80% of the population). This lack of popular support for the Bolsheviks is illustrated further by the fact that they only gained a quarter of the seats in the Constituent Assembly that was finally elected in January 1918, whilst more than half the seats were won by the Social Revolutionaries.

Even within his own party, Lenin struggled to build support for his plan to seize power. Lenin was utterly single-minded throughout 1917 in his determination that the Bolsheviks should under no circumstances work with the Provisional Government ("a stinking corpse"). He harangued Stalin – editor of the Bolshevik newspaper *Pravda* - in April for arguing the opposite (Stalin quickly fell into line). He browbeat the Central Committee of the Bolshevik Party into voting for revolution in October despite the continued misgivings of Kamenev and Zinoviev who felt that the time was not yet ripe. In this sense, at least, Trotsky was right to describe Lenin as the "engine driver" of the revolution, although the alarm of his passengers is frequently overlooked.

Predictably, given their commitment to a revolutionary vanguard and contempt for mass movements, the final military takeover by the Bolsheviks was in the form of a tightly timetabled coup d'état. Lenin had refused to channel the energy of a popular uprising that Summer (the "July Days") and had fled to Finland after it was crushed and the Provisional Government arrested 800 leading Bolsheviks for their suspected involvement. However, although Fitzpatrick rightly calls this event the "low point of Bolshevik fortunes", things quickly improved: when General Kornilov marched his troops towards Petrograd ostensibly to restore order, Kerensky not only released his political prisoners, but provided them with weapons which helped ensure that the feared "Kornilov Coup" was aborted. From this strengthened position, Leon Trotsky set up the Military Revolutionary Committee which worked closely with the Soviets and the sailors of the Kronstadt naval base to produce a timetable for revolution which would ultimately be carried out with clockwork precision in October 1917.

It is abundantly clear that the Provisional Government was on its knees by October 1917. Political paralysis, military ineptitude and social chaos left it highly vulnerable to attack. Nevertheless, if there was a 'party of the people' in 1917 it was not the Bolsheviks, but the Social Revolutionaries. However, their prevarication and continual refusal to seize power for themselves meant that they were increasingly tainted by association with the Provisional Government. The Bolsheviks, as the only party which had from the outset refused to support the war and which called instead for "Peace, Bread and Land" and "All Power to the Soviets" was therefore able to take power in the name of the people, although the reality was that "All Power to the Soviets" was merely a cynical slogan to justify their actions before it became clear that their real objective was "All Power to the Bolsheviks". This was a coup d'état, not a popular uprising, and one which ultimately became what Orlando Figes has famously called a "People's Tragedy" for the Russian nation.

General Hindenburg, Kaiser Wilhelm II and General Ludendorff, Germany general headquarters, February 1917

2. WHY WAS GERMANY DEFEATED ON THE WESTERN FRONT IN WORLD WAR ONE?

With the benefit of hindsight, it is tempting to treat the defeat of Germany at the end of World War One as a historical inevitability: she was encircled by hostile powers and outnumbered in terms of men and war supplies from the outset of the conflict in 1914. However, despite these realities, Germany not only fought her enemies to a standstill over the next four years, but also launched a Spring Offensive in 1918 that came breathtakingly close to dividing the Allied armies and delivering total victory on the Western Front. Such was the disarray within the Allied forces that General Haig issued a desperate rallying cry: "with our backs to the wall and believing in the justice of our cause each one of us must fight on to the end". Nevertheless, just a few months later the Kaiser, Germany's head of state, had fled into exile, his armies were in a state of total disintegration, and the German government essentially surrendered with an armistice agreement. This dramatic reversal of fortunes can be explained partly by Germany's own weaknesses and mistakes, but also the strengths and successes of her enemies - particularly Britain and the United States.

Perhaps the most obvious reason why Germany was defeated is the failure of its high-risk military strategies. They had gambled everything on a short, sharp war based around the Schlieffen Plan: the idea of invading France through neutral Belgium, knocking her out in a couple of months and then concentrating the entire German war machine against Russia, which Germany and its allies thought to be the greater threat. However, the Schlieffen Plan had been adjusted in the years immediately prior to the war so that less army divisions were concentrated against France. This weakness in the plan made it easier for the Allies to slow down the German advance in the Battle of the Marne, with trench warfare being the end result after the 'race to sea' saw both sides fail to outflank the other. Thereafter, the Germans threw everything they could into other desperate strategies to secure victory. The use of poison gas at Loos and flamethrowers at Verdun hardened Allied resistance to the beastly 'Hun', whilst the United States was drawn into the conflict after Germany sent the Zimmerman Telegram trying to persuade Mexico to declare war on the USA and adopting unrestricted submarine warfare against American shipping that supplied Britain and France.

Despite the fanfare with which it was launched, the ultimate expression of military desperation was the Spring Offensive of 1918, when Germany threw all of her available armies into a gigantic assault on the Western Front. This was in the belief that the economic might of the United States, through its ability to provide virtually limitless quantities of weaponry and fighting men, would soon make defeat inevitable. Although her soldiers made spectacular initial gains in terms of territory, they quickly outran their supply lines due to the desperate state of economic production in Germany by this stage. The campaign ground to a halt as half-starved German soldiers fell ravenously upon

French and British supply depots rather than advance further into enemy territory. By August 1918, the Germans were being driven back to the River Marne – where the British army had originally held them back in 1914. Following the capture of 30,000 German troops over the course of two days, General Ludendorff, leader of the German army, declared the war lost, then reversed his position and demanded that armistice negotiations be broken off, only to resign and flee into exile in Sweden when he was overruled by the Kaiser. Speaking of this turning point, AJP Taylor states that "the real effect of August 8 was psychological: it made the hope in victory vanish, which had led the Germans forward. Until then, the German soldiers had been told that this would be the decisive battle. Now they understood that it was indeed. They did not want victory any more. They only wanted to finish fighting".

In contrast, it is one of the ironies of the conflict that the liberal democracies of France and Britain managed to respond to the demands of total warfare more effectively than authoritarian Germany. In Britain, the dynamic Minister of Munitions, David Lloyd George, oversaw the building of fifty new armaments factories which meant that within a year the production of heavy guns was up by more than 1000%. France lost 40% of its industrial capacity to the German invasion in 1914, but rallied by raising in excess of $6 billion of loans from the international finance markets. In 1917 the United States joined the war against Germany, with the result that by January 1918 a further 50,000 fresh troops were arriving each month. Moreover, by this time the Allies had learned from the bitter mistakes made in the Battles of Verdun and the Somme, perfecting the creeping barrage strategy and successfully coordinating the efforts of artillery, infantry and tanks in effective counter attacks against the Germans. Finally, at the height of the Spring Offensive of 1918, General Haig and Marshall Petain, of Britain and France respectively, crucially put their differences aside and gave overall control of the Allied armies to Marshall Foch, thus preventing their armies from being divided by the Germans.

However, although military factors provide the most obvious reason why Germany lost the war, it was underlying economic conditions that drove them towards such desperate military strategies in the first place. In particular, they lacked the colonial empires of France and Britain. It is true that Germany introduced the War Materials Department (KRA) under the leadership of Walter Rathenau to coordinate war production, which was described by Roger Chickering as "The most successful economic organisation created...during the war". However, the essential fact is that Germany had gambled everything on a short war dictated by the Schlieffen Plan – well aware that she did not have the economic resources of empire which would enable her to win a long war of attrition against Britain, France and Russia, all of which had vast empires for troops and supplies. As a result, Germany imposed no ceiling on war profits, nor did she even tax these profits before 1916, when a national income tax system was finally introduced. As a result, the government could only cover 16% of its costs through taxes, when Britain was able to cover about a third. They therefore printed paper money and sold bonds on the assumption that they would recover their costs in reparations after the war; this created inflation as well as massive debt.

In terms of foodstuffs too, the picture for Germany was bleak. With such a small coastline, the British Navy found it a relatively easy task to impose a blockade. The resulting shortages in Germany, which traditionally imported much of its food, pushed many civilians to starvation. By 1915 Germans were eating *Kriegsbrot* (War Bread) made of potatoes, and by the "Turnip Winter" of 1917, the supply of potatoes had run out and the only real alternative was turnips - which were traditionally used as fodder for livestock. In the words of Avner Offer, "Like an invisible net, the problems of food supply entangled German society and its leadership until the war effort became difficult, then impossible, to sustain". The influenza pandemic which then swept across Europe killed 750,000 malnourished Germans. Ultimately, six times as many civilians died in Germany as in France – despite the latter being the occupied country during the war.

In contrast, Germany's enemies were comparatively strong in an economic sense. To take one example, as an island nation Britain was practically impossible for Germany to blockade effectively. When the Germans unleashed unrestricted submarine warfare in 1917, a convoy system was quickly established to protect food supplies and a voluntary rationing scheme was introduced in Britain later that year, along with a vigorous propaganda drive encouraging people to produce their own food ("Join the Women's Land Army!"). The scheme was made compulsory in 1918 and in his memoirs, Lloyd George claimed - although with characteristic overstatement - that as a result "we were never faced with famine or actual privation". In terms of capital goods, the 1914 Defence of the Realm Act (DORA) enabled the government to control the coal and armaments and encouraged almost a million women into the workforce. By 1917, 80% of all bombshells were being produced by female workers known as "Munitionettes".

Just as economic strengths led to direct military benefits, so too did the military performance of the combatants have direct political results. On the one hand - and somewhat ironically - the military victories of Germany weakened her politically. In particular, the initiative for decision-making quickly passed from the Kaiser and the Reichstag to the generals – and in particular Ludendorff and Hindenburg - early on. More importantly, Germany's defeat of Russia in 1917 actually undermined the German war effort in three ways. Firstly, the final Treaty of Brest Litovsk was so harsh that it steeled the determination of the Allies to fight on until Germany's complete defeat fearing similar treatment. Secondly, because the new Soviet government - which had been sponsored by the Germans to destabilise the Russian autocracy - deliberately hampered negotiations with the result that the German armed forces were not liberated to fight on the Western Front as quickly as they should have been. Thirdly and finally, the communist ideology which was now the official position of Soviet Russia quickly spread into Germany itself and undermined its government: by 1918 Bavaria, for example, had declared itself an independent communist republic under the leadership of Kurt Eisner, creating further tensions and distractions.

On the other hand, the democracies of Britain, France and the USA responded robustly to the political centralisation required by the war. In France, party politics were put to one side in favour of patriotism under the banner of the *Union Sacrée* (Sacred Union) as from 1914. In the United States, President Wilson's Fourteen Points were cleverly calculated to destabilise the Austro-Hungarian and Ottoman Empires with their promise of self-determination for oppressed national minorities. In Britain, conscription was introduced by the Military Service Act in 1916, and at the end of that year, Lloyd George became Prime Minister of a formidable national coalition of Liberal, Conservative and Labour politicians - "men of push and go", as he put it - who proceeded to meet on an almost daily basis.

The military conduct of the campaigns also affected the sociocultural conditions in each of the combatant nations in terms of morale. The British in particular generated propaganda designed initially to convince the British people that Germany was evil and that the war against her was therefore just. Posters such as "Remember Belgium!" and cinema shorts depicting Germany as a monster bent on world domination all helped to augment Kitchener's "Your country needs YOU!" recruitment drive which in turn meant that by Christmas 1914 Britain had overcome the lack of conscript army by raising a force of 1 million enthusiastic soldiers. However, from 1916, when conscription had removed the need to persuade men to join up and the Battle of the Somme had made it impossible to hide the carnage of the trenches, propaganda focused instead on encouraging civilians to empathize with the terrible conditions being faced by men at the front (The "Battle of the Somme" film by Geoff Malins being a notable example) and to conserve food supplies in the face of U-Boat attacks ("The Kitchen is the Key to Victory!").

Conversely, Germany was always at a disadvantage in the propaganda war because nothing could disguise the fact that Germany had invaded neutral Belgium and declared war on both Russia and France. As a result, she sacrificed the moral high ground and found it very difficult to produce simple, effective propaganda to motivate civilians and soldiers. Military strategies such as the "Rape of Belgium" in 1914 and the attack on Scarborough by Zeppelin "baby-killers" all increased the difficulties of Germany in cultural terms. In *Mein Kampf*, Hitler - who had fought on the Western Front as a corporal - later criticized the tendency of German and Austria comics to depict the French and British soldiers as being weak and cowardly, since this merely bred complacency outside of battle and then a sense of betrayal within it once it became clear that this message was utterly untrue. In this sense German propaganda, he believed, was not merely inefficient but positively damaging to morale. It is, of course, notoriously difficult for historians to measure the impact of propaganda, but the sudden, final collapse of morale in its armies in 1918 perhaps gives an indication of how the German leaders ultimately failed in their battle to win hearts and minds.

Fundamentally, to ask why Germany lost World War One is inherently misleading. Germany did not so much lose the war as the Allies won it; in other words, the strengths, flexibility and successes of the Allies were at least as important as any direct weaknesses, rigidity and failures of Germany. However, whilst the Allies won the war, they lost the peace: the harshness of the Treaty of Versailles meant that Germany nurtured a sense of injustice that not only helped to propel Hitler to power in Germany, but also meant the British adopted a policy of appeasement towards Germany which led directly to the tragedy of a Second World War.

Lenin and Stalin at Gorki, September 1922

3. HOW SUCCESSFUL WAS LENIN AS RULER OF RUSSIA, 1918-1924?

Between 1917 and 1924 the Bolshevik party went through a trial which transformed it from a revolutionary splinter group into a party of government. During that period, it faced intense opposition from a bewildering array of political, military, social and national groups. By the time of Lenin's death, the regime was, despite all the odds, still in power – but at what cost was this success achieved and to what extent was it superficial rather than real?

Politically, Lenin clearly faced overwhelming opposition following his seizure of power in 1917. The Social Revolutionaries – the party of the peasants - had more support in the countryside, whilst the Bolsheviks - the party of the proletariat, or industrial workers – did not command the overwhelming support of the Soviets. Nevertheless, having made so much political capital out of the Provisional Government's failure to call a Constituent Assembly throughout 1917 in order to form a new government, Lenin had no choice but to call elections immediately. For the Bolsheviks, the results were depressingly predictable: they gained barely a quarter of the available seats, whilst the SR's gained almost half. The Assembly met in January 1918. After electing the SR leader Victor Chernov as Chairman, it promptly refused to accept the Bolshevik suggestion that parliamentary democracy be abandoned in favour of a 'dictatorship of the proletariat' through the Soviets.

Given his precarious position, Lenin's response to this setback at first sight appears reckless: he contemptuously dissolved the Assembly, calling this "true democracy" because he knew the needs of the proletariat better than they did themselves. He then expelled opposition parties from the Central Executive Committee and declared that "our party stands at the head of soviet power. Decrees and measures of soviet power emanate from our party". By the time of Lenin's death, political opposition parties had been formally banned and the Bolshevik Party (renamed the Communist Party in 1919) reigned supreme.

The most important cause for Lenin's political triumph was the weakness of his opponents. The Social Revolutionaries in particular had suffered for years from bitter splits over such issues as the validity of terrorism, participation in the Duma, Russia's Parliament, and support for the Provisional Government in 1917. So it was no surprise that when the moment came, they were deeply divided over whether they should participate in the new Bolshevik government. Ultimately, seven leftist Social Revolutionaries joined the government at the end of 1917 and helped to draft the decree which legitimised the seizure of the land by the peasants. This not only exacerbated the divisions in the Social Revolutionary Party, but consolidated the position of the Bolsheviks in the countryside as the party that legally awarded land to the peasants.

The weaknesses of his opponents made it much easier for Lenin to crush them. In summer 1918, a failed rebellion by the SR's in Moscow and an assassination attempt on Lenin persuaded the Bolsheviks to unleash the 'Red Terror'. This was presided over by the CHEKA, a policing force formed shortly after the October Revolution under the leadership of Dzerzhinsky ("we stand for organised terror: this should be frankly stated"). Within months, membership of the Menshevik and SR parties - which failed to respond by creating their own armed wings - had fallen by two thirds. Trotsky argued that "We raise the sword not to enslave or oppress, but to free all from bondage" and Lenin concurred that "There is absolutely no contradiction between Soviet democracy and the exercise of dictatorial powers". In contrast,

Whilst the Constituent Assembly undermined Lenin's political opponents, the peace treaty signed with Germany in March 1918 served to unite his military opponents. Upon seizing power, Lenin was determined to secure "peace at any price"; the war had already brought down the Tsar and the Provisional Government, and if the Bolshevik regime was not to go the same way, then the war needed to end. Moreover, both Lenin and Trotsky felt that with a world revolution around the corner, the treaty would soon be rendered redundant. Realising that this policy was nevertheless controversial, Trotsky played for time, stringing out negotiations for as long as possible in a tactic he called "no peace, no war". Exasperated, the Germans re-invaded Russia and forced the Bolsheviks to move their capital from Petrograd to Moscow before they eventually signed the Treaty of Brest-Litovsk. Under this punitive treaty, Russia ceded Finland, the Baltic states and Poland - a million square kilometres of territory containing 80% of her coal mines and 30% of her population. Even within the Bolshevik party, the treaty was deeply unpopular; Lenin secured its ratification by the Central Committee only by threatening resignation, and even then by only a majority of one.

Given the unpopularity of the Treaty within Lenin's Bolshevik party, it is hardly surprising that it united anti-Bolshevik military forces. Three 'White Army' commanders posed a serious threat to the Bolshevik regime based around Moscow: Kolchak attacked from the East, Denikin from the South, and Yudenitch from the West. This movement, which had in total over 250,000 troops, was united by a hatred of the Bolsheviks and a desire to restart the war against Germany. This latter objective won them the support of Russia's former allies, who invaded Russia themselves: Britain and France took control of Murmansk and Archangel in the North, whilst the Americans attacked from the Far East, helping Japan to take control of Vladivostok. At one stage, the Bolsheviks had lost control of almost 75% of Russia. However, against what appeared to be overwhelming odds, by spring 1920 all three enemy armies had been defeated.

One reason for the military success of the Bolsheviks is that the Whites had no common cause and so were deeply divided. Moreover, many of the White generals (for example, Denikin and Kolchak) hated each other and so their patriotic rallying cry of 'Russia: one and indivisible' was both hopelessly vague and utterly hypocritical given their reliance on foreign aid. In contrast, the Bolsheviks were united under the leadership of Lenin, who pragmatically reinstated 48,000 experienced Tsarist officers. He in turn was ably supported by Trotsky, who covered 65,000 miles in his mobile train headquarters inspiring the Bolshevik Red Army, which eventually numbered over 5 million disciplined and motivated soldiers.

Secondly, the Bolsheviks possessed a geographical advantage. Firstly, their position in the compacted heartland of Russia gave them a strategic advantage. It not only made it easier for them to coordinate their defence, but also gave them the largest chunk of the population and most of the war industry. Moscow and Petrograd stayed in Bolshevik hands for the entire Civil War, and the symbolic importance of this fact was expressed by the White leader Lebedev, who said that "In Moscow, we would get the whole brain of our country, all her soul, all that is talented in Russia." In contrast, the three main White armies were located at opposite ends of Russia – Denikin and Kolchak were 10,500 kilometres apart and had to communicate via Paris.

Finally, Lenin handled the issue of national minorities more effectively than the Whites. By 1918, there were thirty-three sovereign governments in Russia, but whereas the population of the Russian heartland controlled by the Reds was ethnically homogenous, their opponents needed the support of national minorities, which was awkward given their slogan of "Russia, one and indivisible". In contrast, Lenin denounced the Tsarist empire as "a prison of nations" and promoted the idea of self-determination in the hope that national minorities would vote to stay part of the new Union of Soviet Socialist Republics. However, when it became clear that the national minorities were not going to be persuaded into supporting Bolshevism, Lenin was persuaded by Stalin and others that they would have to be beaten into submission instead. By 1921, the Bolsheviks had regained control of Ukraine, Azerbaijan, Armenia and Georgia. However, Finland and the Baltic states of Latvia, Lithuania, and Estonia declared independence and Marshal Pilsudski secured Polish independence in the Treaty of Riga in March 1921.

The Civil War created further economic dislocation and

pushed Lenin towards a drastic policy called "War Communism" including the rapid nationalisation of all industry, taking control away from the workers, and the requisitioning of all "surplus" food from the peasants. Whilst this succeeded in meeting the immediate needs of the Bolshevik state, it created deep resentment in both the proletariat and the peasantry which eventually escalated into outright rebellion.

The peasantry, at the outset of the Civil War, preferred Lenin's programme of peace, land and worker control to that of the Whites, who wanted to restart the war with Germany and resisted both land reform and worker's rights. Four out of five peasants conscripted into the White armies promptly deserted. However, by early 1918 the honeymoon was over. Chronic food shortages in Petrograd and Moscow pushed the Bolsheviks towards a policy of requisitioning all surplus grain. In 1918 over 7,000 members of requisition squads were murdered, and during 1920 and 1921 a number of violent peasant uprisings occurred in the Ukraine, the Urals, and western Siberia, all suppressed with large concentrations of Red Army troops.

The proletariat provided the key to solving the problem of the peasantry since it could provide the countryside with the industrial goods it needed, which would then give them an incentive to deliver foodstuffs for the towns and the army. Initially, the proletariat formed the bedrock of Bolshevik support and Lenin used workers' factory committees as a means of directing economic policy. However, the economic crisis convinced Lenin to introduce compulsory labour for all citizens and limited the influence of the Soviets by setting up a Supreme Council of the National Economy (*Vesenkha*). This rapidly evolved into an organ of the state staffed by former bourgeois specialists ("knowledgeable, experienced, businesslike people").

On the one hand, Lenin's nationalization of industry and the efforts of Vesenkha to control and coordinate the economy enabled the Bolsheviks to organize munitions production and army supply much better than the Whites. This in itself was a considerable achievement and an essential ingredient of Bolshevik victory. On the other hand, the withdrawal of support for the soviets was ideologically divisive. Economically too, Vesenkha was powerless to counteract the reduction in food, raw materials, and fuel resulting from the loss of control over the Ukraine, the Caucasus, and Central Asia. Total industrial production continued to fall until 1920, when Russian industry produced approximately 14% of what it had in 1913.

By 1921, Lenin's policy of War Communism had brought the country to the verge of chaos. In the countryside, around 6 million peasants had died of starvation and reports circulated in the foreign press that mothers were tying their children to opposite corners of their huts for fear that they would eat each other. In Moscow and Petrograd, thousands of workers went on strike in February 1921, blaming the Bolsheviks for "fraud, theft and all criminality". However, it was the Kronstadt naval rebellion in March 1921 that gave the regime its greatest scare and destroyed its credibility to the greatest degree. The Kronstadt sailors had been described as "the pride and joy of the revolution" by Trotsky, as they had helped overthrow the Provisional Government in 1917 and crushed opposition to the dissolution of the Constituent Assembly the following year. In 1921, however, 16,000 soldiers and workers signed a petition calling for "Soviets without Bolsheviks".

Though the rebellions were mercilessly crushed, Lenin compared the communist state to a man "beaten to within an inch of his life" and, describing Kronstadt as "the flash which lit up reality better than anything else" promptly replaced War

Communism with the New Economic Policy (NEP). This permitted private ownership of small-scale industry and ended grain requisitioning in favour of a tax in kind (eventually settled at 10% of the harvest), with peasants able to sell their surpluses on the open market. By the end of 1922, the crisis began to ease, and by 1923 grain production had increased by 50%.

However, whilst agriculture recovered rapidly, industry did not. Therefore, whilst agricultural prices fell, industrial prices continued to rise. This meant that farmers could not afford to buy industrial goods and were tempted back towards subsistence farming. By the time of the Twelfth Party Congress in 1923, industrial prices were running at three times the level of agricultural prices and Trotsky compared the growing gap between agricultural and industrial prices to the blades of a pair of scissors.

By Lenin's death, industry was well on the way to recovery and the economic "scissors crisis" was largely over, but socially the policy remained deeply divisive. Rumours circulated that NEP really stood for "New Exploitation of the Proletariat", many of whom remained frustrated with the slow progress towards socialism and detested the new breed of enterprising peasants (*kulaks*) and the traders known as Nepmen.

In political terms, its transformation from a party of revolutionary opposition to one of beleaguered government had a profound impact upon the Bolshevik Party. Within months of taking power, debate and internal democracy became an impossible luxury. By 1921, the official instrument of government - Sovnarkom – had been sidelined by the smaller and more cohesive Politburo, which lay at the heart of a single-party state which dealt with dissent through summary executions during the Civil War. As Steve Smith puts it, the crisis of the Civil War was characterised "as much by certain principles being jettisoned as about others being confirmed".

Consequently, the growing power of the state only served to aggravate divisions within the Bolshevik Party. During the period of War Communism, the Workers' Opposition - led by Shiliapnikov and Kollantai - opposed the reduction in the power of the trade unions and the Soviets. Moreover, another Bolshevik faction known as the Democratic Centralists resented the "dictatorship of party officialdom" and had called for more involvement in the decision-making process by rank-and-file Bolsheviks.

Lenin's Decree on Party Unity (1921) banned formal factions, but his partial revival of capitalism in the NEP that same year created still deeper divisions. The right-wing of the party vigorously defended the gradual, peasant-based socialism of the NEP; they were led by Bukharin, who encouraged peasants to "enrich yourselves through the NEP". However, the left-wing Communists quickly came to feel that more emphasis needed to be placed on a programme of rapid industrialization; they were led by Trotsky, who described the NEP as "the first sign of the degeneration of Bolshevism". Lenin tried his best to keep the two wings of the party together by refusing to make clear whether the NEP was a short-term tactical retreat or represented a radical rethinking of communism, but this merely postponed rather than avoided internal party conflict.

In conclusion, by 1922 - the year the USSR was formally proclaimed - it was clear that Lenin had succeeded in dealing with the immediate threats which it had faced upon taking power. However, over the course of that year, Lenin suffered three strokes which left him partially paralysed and politically incapacitated. This served to highlight the cost at which success had been bought. As principles had been compromised and policies had become inconsistent, the Bolsheviks had become so divided that Lenin had dispensed with debate and democracy and relied upon brute force and personal dictatorship to hold the regime together. In the short term, this meant that the party rapidly fragmented following his illness, allowing Stalin to play factions off against each other in order to secure his own ascendancy. In the longer term, it set a tragic ideological precedent which the 'Man of Steel', Stalin, was to exploit with disastrous effects for the state in the years following Lenin's death. Far from "withering away" as Marx had envisaged, the state had become all-powerful. Lenin had replaced one dictatorship with another.

The famous "Lord Kitchener" recruitment poster by Alfred Leete (1914)

4. WHAT WAS THE SOCIAL AND ECONOMIC IMPACT OF WORLD WAR ONE UPON BRITAIN?

The Great War of 1914-1918 was one of the defining events of the 20th century. Its geopolitical results are relatively straightforward to quantify: the overthrow of monarchies in Germany, Austro-Hungary, the Ottoman Empire and Russia; the creation of new nation states such as Poland, Yugoslavia and Czechoslovakia; the weakening of France and Britain and the emergence of the USA as a world power; the creation of the League of Nations. However, the terms of the peace treaties and constitutional re-arrangements only touch upon the deep-seated social and economic changes experienced in combatant nations such as Britain. A consideration of medicine and surgery, the arts, and women's rights provide a deeper understanding of social changes caused or at least accelerated by the war; similarly, government policy towards capital goods on the one hand, and consumer produce on the other, provide the best means of appreciating the economic impact of the war upon the country.

Industrialised warfare created unprecedented challenges for medicine and surgery. There were developments in the recognition and treatment of "shellshock", now known as post-traumatic stress disorder. Most notably, Major Arthur Hurst pioneered therapy treatments at Seale Hayne hospital in Devon where he cured an estimated 90% of soldiers using dietary treatments and therapy sessions. Moreover, the facial reconstruction work of Harold Gillies at Sidcup was the forerunner of modern plastic surgery. Gillies eventually carried out 11,000 operations on over 5,000 men hideously disfigured by shrapnel injuries, enabling them to live relatively normal lives. Many other developments in battlefield surgery also took place. English chemist Henry Drysdale Dakin developed a chlorine-based antiseptic to tackle the threat of gangrene infection; Belgian doctor Albert Hustin pioneered the conservation of blood for transfusion purposes through the addition of citrate; American surgeon George Crile promoted the use of nitrous oxide as an anaesthetic; and the French scientist Marie Curie equipped several hundred vehicles with X-ray machines which helped an estimated one million wounded men over the course of the war.

Nevertheless, the degree of progress should not be overstated. Within the British military, shellshock was often equated with spinelessness and over 300 British soldiers were shot for cowardice. Others were given "Field Punishment Number One" by being strapped to the barrels of heavy artillery guns or other stationary objects as a punishment for up to two hours per day over several weeks. Even sympathetic doctors were unable to explain the condition – arguing, for example, that bursting shells created a vacuum in the brain, and "treating" victims by subjecting them to solitary confinement and electric shock treatment.

In Britain, the arts experienced a drastic shift of focus over the course of the conflict. Propaganda films focused on the evils of

Germany by re-enacting German atrocities in Belgium and their execution of the British nurse Edith Cavell, whom they had accused of spying. Poetry too presented the war as a noble stand against a tyrannical enemy: Rupert Brooke's *The Soldier* ("There is some corner of a foreign field that is forever England") to Laurence Binyon's *For the Fallen* ("Age shall not weary them, nor the years condemn") romanticised those killed in battle as heroic immortals.

However, 1916 was a turning point. The introduction of conscription in Britain meant that propaganda no longer needed to encourage men to join the army, and the Battle of the Somme made it impossible to hide the murderous reality of war. Suddenly, government propaganda films (for example, Malins' *Battle of the Somme*) began highlighting rather than downplaying the horror of the Western Front to encourage the civilians back home to give their support to men on leave rather than trivialise their experiences. A similar shift occurred in the visual arts. Mark Gertler's *Merry Go Round* references the widely held fear that the war would go on forever; Christopher Nevinson's *Machine Gun* presents soldiers as mechanised drones inseparable from the weapons they operate; and Paul Nash's *We are Making a New World* depicts the devastated landscape of the Western Front in uncompromising terms ("I am no longer an artist, I am a messenger to those who want the war to go on for ever ... and may it burn their lousy souls").

Poetry too shifted in tone: an early idealist such as Wilfred Owen started to produce dark, bitter poems such as *Dulce et Decorum Est* ("If you could hear, at every jolt, the blood / Come gargling from the froth-corrupted lungs") whilst hardened cynics such as Siegfried Sassoon's *Suicide in the Trenches* raves against the futility of war ("You smug-faced crowds...sneak home and pray you'll never know the hell where youth and laughter go"). Despite this, we should not overstate the clarity of the shift from idealism to cynicism, for the reality was that many of those involved retained a confused opinion about the war throughout. Nowhere is this more clear than in the poem *In Flanders Fields* by John McRae, which starts as a tragic paean to the young war dead ("Short hours ago we...loved and were loved") but ends as a jingoistic call to arms ("Take up our quarrel with the foe").

If we turn to the impact of World War One upon women in Britain, the effects were in some ways clearly positive. Before the conflict, the notion of 'separate spheres' insisted that women belonged at home, men at work. Despite high-profile and increasingly violent campaigns, the suffragettes had therefore failed to secure the vote for women. During the war, however, the suffragettes called off their campaign and threw their support behind the war effort. Many women flocked to join the "Women's Land Army" to help increase food production in the countryside, whilst thousands of others went to work as "Munitionettes" in the armaments factories. Overall, the number of women as a percentage of the working population rose from 24% in 1914 to between over 40% in 1918 and many women found this, in the words of Gail Braybon, a "genuinely liberating experience". After the war, having proven themselves to be politically responsible and economically vital, many women were given the vote in the Representation of the People Act (1918). The new-found independence of women expressed itself not only in the "Flapper" fashions of the "Roaring 20s" Jazz Age, but through a new openness towards sexuality, for example with Marie Stopes in England promoting contraception and family planning in her book *Married Love*.

However, the picture for women was not completely progressive, despite the claim by the suffragist Millicent Fawcett that "it found women serfs and left them free". Many women worked in hazardous conditions: 200 British Munitionettes died in factory explosions – the worst disaster being at the Silvertown factory - and countless other "canaries" (so called for their yellowish pallor caused by the dangerous chemicals they worked with) suffered the disfigurement of "Phossy [phosphorous] Jaw". Economically, employers circumvented wartime equal pay regulations by employing several women to replace one man, or by dividing skilled tasks into several less-skilled stages. In these ways, women could be employed at a lower wage and not said to be 'replacing' a man directly. By 1931, a working woman's weekly wage had returned to the pre-war situation of being half the male rate in more industries. Politically, the vote was only given to women at the age of 30 (as opposed to 21 for men) who owned a substantial amount of property. According to Deborah Tom, "the war had not challenged the sexual division of labour or the notion of the male bread-winner. These roles were only suspended for the duration and then only in some households".

For Britain as for other belligerent nations, the war also had serious economic implications. Within a few months of the outbreak of the conflict it became clear that it would not be "all over by Christmas" but would instead be a grinding war of attrition. Victory would go to the side not with the greatest military might, but with the greatest ability to mobilise its economic resources to the demands of "total war". In Britain, the conflict witnessed a centralisation of government economic control in the interests of efficiency. The 1914 Defence of the Realm Act (DORA) gave the government powers over both the bosses (with regards to what was to be produced) and employees (with regards to where they were to work). The Munitions Crisis of 1915 led to the provisions of DORA being vigorously implemented: the government took over control of the coal and armaments industries, and almost a million women were recruited into the workforce. The government stepped up another gear following the German declaration of unrestricted submarine warfare in 1917, which in March of that year resulted in the sinking of 500,000 tons of merchant shipping. A convoy system was quickly established to protect food supplies and a rationing scheme was successfully introduced.

Nevertheless, the superficial impression created of government, bosses and workers united against a common enemy masked a much tenser reality. Industrial relations had been bad before the war – as reflected in a national coal strike of 1912, for example – and the government continued to face a number of unofficial strikes throughout the war, most notably of the metalworkers on the Clyde in Glasgow (1915) and of the Amalgamated Society of Engineers (1917, 1918). The government had no choice but to capitulate to the demands of the unions, which had become unprecedentedly powerful as a result of the war. The long-term economic impact of the war was also deeply damaging. Correlli Barnett has argued that "in objective truth the Great War in no way inflicted crippling economic damage on Britain" but this is debatable. By 1918, the war had cost Britain £11 billion (£7 million per day by 1917), much of which was borrowed from the USA. Interest payment on loans represented 40% of annual government spending, as opposed to 12% in 1913. 40% of her merchant shipping had been sunk by U-Boats. According to Niall Ferguson, this "represents the beginning of British decline" and meant that Britain lost its status as "The World's Banker" to the USA.

The coal industry was particularly badly affected. During the war many of Britain's natural markets had dried up as countries found alternative sources of supply in the distorted international situation. After the war, the mine owners sought to compensate for their smaller profits by lengthening working hours and cutting rates of pay. This led to a worsening of labour relations. Employers and unions had clashed on numerous occasions throughout the conflict and the government had frequently played a mediating role, but following the defeat of Germany the government rapidly lost the support of the unions for two main reasons. Firstly, Lloyd George was too slow to deliver the "homes fit for heroes" he had promised in the "coupon election" of 1918. Secondly, Churchill had caused economic hardship by returning Britain to the Gold Standard at the wrong rate (in a misguided attempt to counteract the resurgence of the German economy following the Dawes Plan of 1924). It was against this background that the Trades Union Congress (TUC) called a devastating General Strike in 1926. Although eventually crushed by the government, the bitterness and injustice that inspired it remained intact.

Overall, in social terms the war caused some rapid changes in Britain: medicine and surgery and women's rights in particular clearly saw some notable advances. Economically, one of the ironies of the war is that Liberal England adapted to the centralising necessities of "total war" much more effectively than authoritarian Germany, although in terms of labour relations it is a propaganda myth to suggest that the war led to a temporary truce in the disputes between bosses and workers that had characterised the pre-war period. The deepest long-term change caused by the war, however, was the fact that Britain was left economically bankrupt by the war at the very point that society was demanding its greatest support.

Portrait of Benito Mussolini in the 1930s

5. HOW SUCCESSFULLY DID MUSSOLINI ESTABLISH FASCISM IN ITALY?

The fundamental challenge for any historian measuring the degree to which Mussolini achieved his objectives in Italian domestic policy is that Fascism never had a coherent philosophy. Unlike Nazism, which had Hitler's *Mein Kampf*, and communism, which had a plethora of writings from Marx, Engels and Lenin, Mussolini never produced an extended exposition about the Fascist ideology he formulated. Indeed, many historians would argue that the defining feature of Fascism is the fact that it is essentially anti-ideological; it was not so much a political creed as a nebulous 'Third Way' between capitalism and communism. Nevertheless, through his speeches and writings it remains possible to identify some central tenets of Fascism against which Mussolini's policies can be judged.

One key feature of Fascism is that it is rabidly anti-democratic. Mussolini aimed to establish totalitarian control over the political system through the creation of a one-party state. Having come to power in 1922 as the leader of a coalition government, this was Mussolini's most immediate objective. In 1923 he pushed the Acerbo Law through Parliament, giving two-thirds of the Parliamentary seats to whichever party gained more than one-quarter of the vote. When the socialist leader Matteotti was killed by Fascists the following year (shortly after delivering a blistering speech against their political corruption), Mussolini accepted "moral" responsibility for the murder and skilfully turned it to his advantage by using Italy's culture of violence to justify passing a new censorship law and to later ban opposition parties.

Mussolini's success in this area, however, was less due to his own strengths than to the weaknesses of his opponents who stormed out of Parliament (an event known as the 'Aventine Secession') in protest and thereby left it in his hands at the height of the Matteotti Crisis. A more direct failure was that the King remained firmly in place throughout Mussolini's rule. Mussolini was appointed by constitutional means, and dismissed by constitutional means in 1943. In this sense, and despite his desperate attempts to depict the March on Rome as a violent takeover rather than a stage-managed media event, he never established a true Fascist dictatorship.

The other great barrier to the creation of genuine totalitarian control was religious rather than political – the Roman Catholic Church. In ideological terms, Mussolini (a lifelong atheist who called priests 'black germs') saw the Church as an alternative belief system. Nevertheless, pragmatically Mussolini recognized that his regime, to be stable, would have to reach out to the Vatican – after all, 99% of Italians belonged to the Catholic church. On this basis he recognized the Church as being a "source of pride for all us Italians". He signed the Lateran Treaties with the Papacy, under which the Pope was compensated for the loss of papal lands during the formation of the Italian state and in return he recognized the legitimacy of the Italian state. This was perhaps Mussolini's most immediate and most lasting practical achievement, but as well as being ideologically unsound, it was a practical failure in the mid-term: Mussolini resented the continued influence of the Pope's youth organisation "Catholic Action", whilst the Pope bitterly condemned the antisemitic policies (in *The Manifesto of the Italian Race*) pursued by Mussolini after he fell under the thrall of Hitler in 1938.

Mussolini's failure to establish totalitarian control over the monarchy and the church meant that he placed a great deal of emphasis upon the creation of a cult of personality around himself, presenting himself as the unrivalled *Duce* (leader) of Italy. He set up the Ministry of Popular Culture (*Miniculpop*) which involved itself in every area of the media. The newspaper *Popolo D'Italia* publicised positive assessments of Mussolini by foreign statesmen such as Churchill and Austen Chamberlain (who called Mussolini a "wonderful man") and a million cheap radio sets were sold and broadcast the Fascist "Chronicles of the Regime". Through this, Mussolini was depicted as a demigod: a soldier, aviator, musician, intellectual par excellence who modestly stated in one interview that "Often I would like to be wrong, but so far it has never happened".

Whilst it is difficult to determine exactly how many people actually believed this propaganda, there were some concrete victories which helped Italians to overcome the sense of disappointment that had come out of the wreckage of World War One: in the 1932 Olympics, "Mussolini's Boys" won twelve gold medals, and in 1934 the World Cup was hosted and won by Italy. Nevertheless, the rapidity with which Mussolini's reputation crumbled after he took Italy into World War Two – not to mention the ignominious end of having his bullet-ridden corpse strung upside-down at an Esso petrol station – provides stark evidence that the "Cult of Ducismo" was never as deeply rooted as he believed.

A second way in which Mussolini aimed to counteract the continued power of the monarchy and the church was to develop a whole new conception of the state. Rather than merely being a tool to get things done, the state would be seen as a focus of nationalistic pride and devotion ("All within the state, nothing outside the state, nothing against the state… the State is absolute, individuals and groups relative"). The clearest expression of this idea was the formation of a 'Corporate State' in which the interests of all social classes would be equally represented ("Fascism should more appropriately be called Corporatism because it is a merger of state and corporate power"). Like Hitler later, Mussolini banned the 'communistic' trade union movement in the Vidoni Pact in 1925 and replaced it with a system of syndicates in the Rocco Laws in 1926. Each major industry was to have one body to represent the workers, one to represent the employers, all of which were under the general auspices of a Ministry of Corporations. Although in reality the employers had more rights than the workers because they could choose their own representatives rather than have them appointed by the state, Mussolini was able to gloss over this anomaly by providing the workers with subsidised holidays and leisure facilities through the *Dopolovaro* organisation. This is perhaps one of Mussolini's most notable achievements, copied by Roosevelt, amongst others, as part of his 'New Deal' programme.

A rampant Italian nationalism which glorified violence and conflict was the central message that the new Fascist state aimed to inculcate into its people through the *Duce* cult and the Corporate State ("Fascism…believes neither in the possibility nor the utility of perpetual peace"). To rebuild the glories of the

Roman Empire (Mussolini often compared himself to Caesar), the *Duce* needed soldiers – lots of them – and Mussolini was therefore determined to double the country's population within a generation ("All nations and all empires first felt decadence gnawing at them when their birth rate fell off"). Marriage grants were provided to young couples, part of which was written off with each new child born; families with six or more children were tax-exempt, contraception was banned, and a "Bachelor Tax" was imposed on single people. However, although Mussolini believed that "a woman's place is in the home and preferably pregnant", these policies were a triumph of style over substance. The birth rate actually fell in the 1930s, and during World War Two Mussolini complained that this had cost him the equivalent of 15 army divisions.

Another key tenet of Fascism, connected to the belief in the desirability of warfare, was a desire to establish totalitarian control over the economy in order to ensure that in time of war it would not be held to ransom by the international markets. Agriculturally, Mussolini's policies met with some success as the "Battle for Grain" doubled Italy's grain production, whilst the land reclamation programme in the Pontine Marshes was a propaganda coup for the Duce, who took every opportunity to strip to the waist and get involved in the work (at least, whenever the cameras were present). However, these policies delivered few tangible economic benefits for ordinary people, benefitting instead the large landowners – and much of the land used for grain production would have been much better suited to citrus crops. Financially his policies were not merely ineffectual, but downright damaging. The "Battle for Lira", for example, raised the exchange rate for the Italian currency which was an ill-considered act of bravado which killed the Italian export boom and which ultimately had to be reversed. By the 1930s he was openly admitting defeat, bluntly stating that "We are probably moving towards a lower standard of living" (1936) but that "fortunately the Italian people were not accustomed to eat much and therefore feel the privation less than others"!

To conclude, assessing Mussolini's success in Fascist terms is difficult since within each policy he had to balance his ideological preferences with practical realities. His most lasting practical achievement – the solution of the church-state dispute – was arguably the most ideologically unsound of his policies since it gave grudging support to an alternative belief system. The regime's emphasis on appearances and prestige rather than concrete achievements meant that Italy was not prepared socially, economically or politically when Mussolini led her into war in 1940. The consequences of this became almost immediately apparent and had a catastrophic effect for the Italian people, and fatal consequences for Mussolini himself.

Prime Minister Azaña driving a steamroller over his right-wing enemies: cover of *La Traca* magazine, April 1932

6. WHAT WERE THE CAUSES OF THE SPANISH CIVIL WAR?

The Spanish Civil War (1936-1939) was a tragedy which cost upwards of 300,000 lives and which culminated in the victory of General Franco, who ruled as a military dictator until his death in 1975. It was fundamentally the result of long-term socio-economic weaknesses which provided fuel for aggressively ambitious regionalist movements. Arguments about how to deal with these problems created deep political divisions which were sharpened further by debates over religion. The military stepped into the power vacuum thereby created to impose a violent solution for its own long-standing grievances. The failure of this coup condemned the country to a three-year civil war.

The immediate cause of the Spanish Civil War was the failure of the military coup against the Second Republic led by Generals Mola, Sanjurjo and Franco. This gave the Republican government sufficient breathing space to mount a counter-assault that led the country into a protracted civil war. The causes for the failure of the coup can be at least partly explained by the fact that the Republic, far from being an unpopular failure, had a number of notable achievements which gave it a bedrock of support among the industrial proletariat and liberal progressives in particular. For example, the Labour Arbitration Scheme which had been introduced before the Second Republic by the dictator Primo de Rivera to settle disputes between workers and bosses had been extended and improved. In religious terms, the reactionary Jesuit Order of the Catholic Church was dissolved, the state withdrew Church subsidies and banned religious education. Civil marriage was permitted and divorce was allowed, both previously the monopoly of the Church. Partly as a result of such broadly popular reforms, Prime Minister Manuel Azaña had been able to defeat with ease the earlier military revolt by General Sanjurjo in 1932.

Nevertheless, if the divisions within Spanish society explain why the rebellion was unable to secure its objectives in 1936, they also explain why the coup was organised in the first place. The underlying cause of these tragic divisions can be found in deep socio-economic weaknesses that created increasing tensions in the years leading up the crisis. Socially, poverty for the peasantry and the proletariat were nothing new, as illustrated by the bloodshed of "Tragic Week" (1909). During the Primo regime, resistance of the landowners meant that Finance Minister Sotelo failed to reform the tax system; this meant reliance on foreign loans and credit to operate the government, leaving the country more vulnerable to the effects of the Great Depression after 1929. Skyrocketing unemployment resulted from agricultural prices plummeting and industrial production collapsing by up to 50%. The social distress resulting from this was exacerbated by the fact that Primo de Rivera's arbitration scheme did not extend to rural areas due to landowner opposition. The advent of the Second Republic raised unrealistic hopes that were perhaps inevitably unfulfilled. The Asturias Uprising of 1934 saw coal miners launch a general strike which was ruthlessly put down by an army led by General Franco (who became known as 'The Butcher of Asturias'); two thousand people were killed and tens of thousands went to prison. In the countryside, the Agrarian Reform Law (1932) allowed the state to nationalise the largest privately-owned farms (the *Latifundia*), and then hand them over to the peasants; however, compensating the landowners was complicated and expensive, and the government was divided on the issue of collectivisation and so it was never implemented on a large scale. Consequently, it angered the landowners yet disappointed the peasants too. Many peasants increasingly supported the anarchists, who encouraged the peasants to take over the land by force if necessary - for example, in March 1936, 60,000 landless anarchist workers took over 3000 farms in Extramadura.

Socio-economic injustices provided fuel for aggressively ambitious regionalist movements which threatened Spain's unity. Regionally, Catalonia and the Basque country demanded self-government; they were more industrially advanced than the rest of Spain and they felt they were being held back and exploited by the rest of the country. Primo de Rivera's initial approach had been to create a Catalan regional assembly and to promote a policy of tolerance towards Basque and Catalan literature in schools. However, these early concessions were withdrawn, and the Catalonian flag was banned when it became clear that the new assembly would not be a bulwark of support for the Primo regime. The Second Republic gave Catalonia home rule in 1932, which proved popular in the region itself but controversial in the rest of Spain.

Heated political debates took place not just on issues of socio-economic policy and demands for regional independence, but also on matters of religion, which in turn served to create even deeper political divisions. The Catholic Church had a stranglehold over education since the 1851 Concordat and benefited from vast public subsidies. With its emphasis on tradition, order and discipline, it not only supported the rights of the landowners over those of the peasantry, but also the rights of the military over the forces of democracy and reform. All this meant that ordinary Spaniards regarded the Catholic Church with a strange mixture of reverence and hatred - an old saying was that "Spaniards follow their priests either with a candle or a club". Anticlericalism - opposition to the power of the Church hierarchy - was therefore the strongest common ground of all Republicans; indeed, convents were spontaneously attacked only a month after the Republic was proclaimed in April 1931 and the radical new government did nothing to stop this, with Azaña stating that "all the convents in Spain were not worth the life of a single Republican". In reaction to this, the conservative Gil Robles formed the CEDA party (*Confederación Española de Derechas Autónomas* or Spanish Confederation of Autonomous Rights) to protect the interests of the Roman Catholic Church and its supporters.

Arguments about how to deal with these problems created deep political divisions - not just between Left- and Right-wing parties, but also within them. This meant that no single party was able to form a strong government by gaining a majority of seats in the Parliament. Instead, a series of short-lived coalition governments were formed, each of which pursued its own radical reforms and reversed those of its predecessor. This meant that little progress was made but a great deal of bitterness was created. For example, the "Left Republic" led by Azaña (1931-1933) was overthrown by the "Right Republic" led by Robles (1933-35). In 1936, this in turn was overthrown by the extreme Left-wing "Popular Front" government, which led to Right-wing parties joining forces in a reactionary alliance called the "National Front". The final spark was provided by the murder of Finance Minister Sotelo, who had shortly before called for an authoritarian right-wing government to restore order and ended by saying "I declare myself fascist".

Against this backdrop of chaos, incompetence and inconsistency, the military not only stepped into the power vacuum, but also took advantage of the situation to impose a violent solution for its own long-standing grievances. The Spanish Empire was in humiliating decline, most recently following the loss of Cuba (1898) and the defeat in Annual, Spanish Morocco (1921). By the time of the Second Republic, the failure to make corresponding cuts in military staffing meant there was a general for every 11 soldiers. To save money, Azaña passed a controversial law forcing many army officers into early retirement and reviewing upcoming promotions including that of Franco, whose military academy in Zaragoza was also closed down as part of the reductions. The Sanjurjo Rebellion of 1932 was crushed by the army, but as politics grew increasingly polarised, some Left-Wing Republicans, such as Largo Caballero, started to call for a communist revolution. The military leadership was convinced that the country was in serious danger of a communist takeover. On this basis, General Mola was eventually able to persuade General Franco to join the coup against the Republic. He was flown to mainland Spain with his troops, triggering the series of events that would culminate into a civil war.

The fundamental cause of the Spanish Civil War was therefore extreme socio-economic tension which manifested itself on every level of society: deep-seated poverty for the peasantry and the proletariat fuelled demands for radical reforms and regional independence. These in turn were opposed by the reactionary elements in Spain, particularly the Catholic Church, which supported the privileges of the army and the landowners. The failure of politicians from across the political spectrum in Spain to resolve these differences resulted in hundreds of thousands of deaths and untold destruction; the country continues to grapple with many of the legacies of the Civil War even today.

Republican militiawoman in Plaça Catalunya,
Barcelona 1936. Photograph by Gerda Taro (d.1937)

7. WAS THE OUTCOME OF THE SPANISH CIVIL WAR DECIDED BY FOREIGN POWERS?

The Spanish Civil War is often regarded as the forerunner of World War Two – a clash between the forces of democracy and dictatorship, and between Fascism and Communism. As a result, there has been a tendency for historians to view the conflict through the prism of international as much as domestic factors. Hugh Trevor-Roper, for example, said that the war was "decided in the chancelleries of Europe rather than on the battlefields of Spain". More recently, Hugh Thomas describes the war as "an international crisis whose solution was decided by external circumstances" whilst Richard Evans states that "those who regarded the Spanish Civil War as the great European ideological struggle of its time were right to do so". Somewhat ironically, Soviet aid to the Republic was ultimately of more significance in helping Franco to final victory than fascist aid to his Nationalists. However, foreign involvement merely acted as a catalyst for the domestic factors which produced the final outcome of the war.

It is certainly true that the Nationalists received an impressive degree of assistance from foreign powers. Economically, Franco took $700 million from the United States, mainly from Catholic sponsors eager to save Spain from what they believed were godless Republicans. Militarily, Nazi support in "Operation Magic Fire" was crucial in the opening phases of the rebellion, when Hitler provided Franco with 20 transport planes that brought bring his troops back to the Spanish mainland from Morocco (the navy remaining notably loyal to the Republic). Mussolini too sent 60,000 men to help the Nationalist campaign. Moreover, the war planes of Germany not only helped Franco destroy Basque resistance through its attacks on Guernica, but also sent out a terrifying message to other cities in the Nationalist path that Franco and his Fascist backers were not afraid to prosecute a 'total war' against their enemies. Without this assistance, the revolt may well have been over before it began, and after the Nationalist victory Hitler said that Franco should erect a monument to the German planes that had helped him win the war.

However, the importance of aid from foreign powers in ensuring Franco's victory should not be overstated; it could be argued that his association with the Fascists was a hindrance. Mussolini's troops performed badly at the battle of Guadalajara after they refused to integrate with Franco's regular forces, whilst Hitler's decision to bomb Guernica damaged Franco's reputation with many of his own people. At best, therefore, foreign aid to Franco merely compounded his existing strengths, not least amongst which was his ability to stand up to his foreign sponsors and forge his own path. Militarily he refused to march straight on Madrid, preferring instead an 'inch by inch' strategy which exasperated Mussolini and Hitler. Economically, he was happy to sign away 75% of Spain's mining rights to Hitler in the Montana Project, and let Mussolini think that the Balearic Islands might go to Italy after a Nationalist victory, but ultimately refused to deliver on either promise. Franco was his own man, and it was down to his efforts alone that Hitler had been personally persuaded to provide him with assistance. Franco was also aided by the deaths of political rivals such as Jose Antonio (leader of the Fascist Falange party) and the exile of the Carlist leader Fal Conde. This allowed him to declare himself *Caudillo* (political leader) with little opposition, to create the *FET y de las JONS* movement to unite the Nationalists under a clear political banner, and to become *Generalissimo* (military leader) of the Nationalist armies after the deaths of Mola and Sanjurjo. All of this was achieved not because of, but rather sometimes in spite of, the pressures placed on him by his Fascist allies.

From this it ironically follows that Franco's victory in the war was aided more by foreign aid given to the Republic by the USSR than by foreign aid given to the Nationalists by their allies. The USSR provided military assistance in the form of hardware and 500 Soviet military advisors, but this was in return for an up-front payment amounting to three-quarters of Madrid's gold reserves - some $500 million in total. Stalin told his Politburo that "The Spaniards will never see their gold again, just as they don't see their ears". This severely limited the ability of the Republican government under Juan Negrin to deliver on its promise of social reform and economic regeneration due to the resulting financial crisis, and by the middle of the war many Republicans were surviving on a daily ration of lentils (bitterly nicknamed "Dr. Negrin's Resistance Pills").

The problems of the Republic were exacerbated by deep political divisions which meant that its governments were a series of weak coalitions. For example, Negrin's PCE and Caballero's PSOE on the one side followed Stalin's lead in calling for the revolution to be put on hold until the war was won. This meant an end to collectivisation in the countryside and the democratic militias on the battlefront. This pitted them against the Nin's Trotskyist POUM and Durutti's anarchist CNT, who felt that the revolutionary spirit needed to be kept alive if the war was to be won at all. Caballero's insistence on creating a regular "Popular Army" and his order that the militias be disbanded precipitated a "Civil War within the Civil War" in Barcelona in 1937 which sapped the ability of the Republic to defend itself. The parties of the moderate Right were marginalised or drifted towards the Nationalists, leaving the Left-Wing parties to engage in internecine warfare which made effective leadership in the Republican zone highly problematic.

Perhaps most fatally of all, the controversy created in the Republican zone by Negrin's increasingly close association with Stalin's USSR meant that the western democracies of France and Britain refused to budge from their position of neutrality in the civil war. They took an early lead in organising an international Non-Intervention Committee (NIC), which eventually represented 27 states and which effectively condemned the Spanish Republic to political isolation and an economic embargo. Scott Ramsay argues that Britain demonstrated an attitude of "benevolent neutrality", but more cynically it can be argued that non-intervention was due to the fact that the possibility of a communist Spain was even less palatable to the British than one led by Franco's nationalists. Non-intervention also fitted into the broader policy of appeasement that was being pursued by Chamberlain and Daladier in Britain and France respectively: they were willing to turn a blind eye to the support given to Franco by Hitler and Mussolini - both ostensibly member of the NIC - in the hope that this would keep them as a useful bulwark against further Soviet expansion into Europe. When the British Labour leader Clement Attlee criticised the "gross betrayal, [the] hypocritical pretence of non-intervention", foreign secretary Anthony Eden's view was "A leaky dam: better than no dam at all".

In summary, it is clear from the evidence that the outcome of the Spanish Civil War was not determined on the battlefields of Spain, but neither was it determined in the chancelleries of Europe. Rather, it was determined in the chancelleries of Spain itself: in other words, the deep political divisions within the Republic made effective prosecution of the war impossible in the military, social and economic sense. These factors were exacerbated, not caused, by the interference of the USSR; similarly, these factors resulted in, and were not caused by, Britain and France's formation of the Non-Intervention Committee. In this sense, and for all Franco's own talents and achievements, it can be fairly said that the Spanish Civil War was lost by the Republic rather than won by Franco, and that the very lack of involvement by foreign powers was every bit as important as their active contribution.

Benito Mussolini and Adolf Hitler during Mussolini's visit in Munich, June 1940

8. HOW SIMILAR WERE THE FOREIGN POLICIES OF HITLER AND MUSSOLINI?

To the casual observer, Mussolini and Hitler are something of a diabolical double act: aggressive right-wing dictators who rose to power in similar circumstances, shared a similar ideology, fought side by side in World War Two, and died violently at the end of the conflict in 1945. But the reality is much more complex. In particular, it was Mussolini's Italy – not the democracies of Britain, France or the USA – that initially led the most vigorous attempts to contain the aggression of Hitler's Germany. It was the West's decision to appease Hitler rather than confront him that was at least partly responsible for Mussolini's decision to realign Italy as an ally of Germany. In the words of Richard Lamb, "British policy threw Mussolini into Hitler's arms". A study of the foreign policy of both dictators therefore highlights at least as many contrasts as comparisons.

Both Mussolini and Hitler recognized the importance of good relations with the British Empire as a means of advancing the position of their countries. Throughout the 1920s, British foreign policy was dominated by the fear of a resurgent Germany on the one hand, and an aggressive communist Soviet Union on the other. It was on this basis that Britain, along with France, had refused to accept either country as initial members of the League of Nations.

Mussolini's policy was to play upon British fears of a resurgent and vengeful Germany by making strenuous efforts to enforce the Treaty of Versailles. This was true during the Locarno Conference of 1925, when he arrived in a flotilla of speedboats and was described by the British foreign secretary Austen Chamberlain described him as "A good man to do business with". This policy continued into the 1930s. Indeed, it is a misconception that the rise to power of Hitler in Germany in 1933 led Mussolini to adopt a more aggressive, anti-Western policy. Quite the opposite: he initially regarded Hitler as a rival and a "sexual degenerate". Alone among the powers of Europe, Italy stood up to Hitler: in 1934, after the murder of Chancellor Dollfuss of Austria by Nazis, Mussolini sent troops to the Austrian border to threaten invasion and thereby forced Hitler to abandon his plans to annex Austria, the Anschluss which did occur four years later. Mussolini personally arranged the Stresa Pact of 1935 between Italy, France and Britain in which all agreed to stand shoulder to shoulder against any further instances of German expansionism, especially in Austria.

Hitler's policy, in contrast, was to exploit British fears of communist Russia and thereby secure a revision of the Treaty of Versailles in Germany's favour. When Hitler became Chancellor in January 1933, Germany was on good terms with the Soviet Union; the two countries had come together in the Rapallo Treaty of 1922 after both had lost territory to Poland after World War One and had been denied entry into the League by France and Britain. Hitler immediately revoked the Rapallo Treaty and then signed a treaty of friendship with Poland, Russia's bitterest enemy. This firm stance against communism impressed the

British, who signed the Anglo-German Naval Agreement with Hitler in 1935, even though this contradicted the terms of the Treaty of Versailles and (as Hitler intended) seriously damaged Britain's standing with her Stresa Pact allies.

Hitler's emphasis of the threat posed by communist Russia was primarily intended to draw Britain in particular closer to Germany, but it had the same effect upon Italy. As fellow Fascists, Mussolini and Hitler genuinely detested Marxism. So, when General Franco led a rebellion in 1936 against the left-wing "Popular Front" government of Spain for pushing Spain towards communism, they were naturally inclined to aid the rebels.

It was during the Spanish Civil War that Mussolini and Hitler became firm allies. Hitler provided essential transport planes that enabled Franco's troops to move from Morocco to Spain in the first moments of the rebellion; thereafter, he formed the Condor Legion that notoriously bombed the Basque city of Guernica. Mussolini ultimately deployed 80,000 Italian soldiers in Spain. Hitler and Mussolini also created the Rome-Berlin Axis (1936) to formulate a common foreign policy to deal with the threat posed by Stalin's Comintern (Communist International). Japan joined shortly afterwards, concerned about Comintern's commitment to world revolution: this could threaten their major province of Manchuria that bordered the USSR, seized earlier from China which also had an armed and violently anti-Japanese communist party. This new Anti-Comintern Pact (1937) formed the basis of the wartime "Axis" alliance between Germany, Japan and Italy. The same year, Mussolini was given a lavish welcome when he paid an official state visit to Germany.

However, although the Spanish Civil War superficially stresses the similarities between the foreign policy of Nazi

Germany and Fascist Italy, it also highlights some differences. Firstly, Hitler saw the war not only as a chance to combat communism and to demonstrate his military power (objectives shared by Mussolini) but also as a chance to increase his economic power: the price he extracted from Franco for continued German aid was the Montana Project (1938), which gave Germany access to 75% of Spanish ores essential for the Nazi war machine. Secondly, Hitler saw the Spanish Civil War as an opportunity to embroil Italy in a conflict which would leave Austria more open to a Nazi takeover. Sure enough, in 1937 Mussolini's troops suffered a massive and humiliating defeat at the Battle of Guadalajara, so the following year Hitler was able to absorb Austria into the Third Reich with none of the opposition he had faced from Italy when he attempted the same manoeuvre in 1934.

The twin themes of prestige and power which highlight similarities and differences between Mussolini and Hitler regarding the Spanish Civil War can also be applied to their imperialistic ventures. Mussolini's imperial policy was more concerned with prestige than with power. Italy had been on the side of the victors in 1918, but her sense of pride had been damaged by the poor gains that she had secured at the Versailles Peace Conference. Brought to power partly due to this sense of affronted nationalism, Mussolini promptly invaded Corfu in 1923. He then focused on the Balkans, securing Fiume, today's Rijeka, from Yugoslavia in 1924 and gradually increasing Italian military and economic influence in Albania until she was formally annexed in 1939. These territories brought prestige but no tangible economic benefits to Italy; this was even more true of Abyssinia, the poverty-stricken nation which Mussolini brutally invaded in 1935. Throughout, Mussolini's actions lend weight to AJP Taylor's conclusion that he was a "vain blundering boaster without either ideas or aims".

Germany's sense of pride had also been affronted by the Treaty of Versailles – in particular, the "War Guilt" clause rankled deeply - but of more concern to Hitler was the loss of power suffered by his country. Throughout the 1930s, his foreign policies methodically rebuilt German strength. The remilitarisation of the Rhineland (1936) strengthened Germany's military position by leaving the *Wehrmacht* positioned on the French border; the Anschluss with Austria (1938) more than compensated for the territorial losses suffered by Germany in 1918. Seizure of the Sudetenland after the Munich Conference (1938) brought the economic heartland of Czechoslovakia under the control of the Third Reich. His invasions of Czechoslovakia and then Poland in 1939 make it quite plain that his desire for raw power easily outweighed any desire to obtain statesmanlike prestige.

Germany's invasion of Poland in 1939 led to a larger European and eventually a world-wide war and the start of a new era in the relationship between Mussolini and Hitler. Mussolini signed the Pact of Steel (1939) with Hitler, committing Italy to joining a war on Germany's side even if Germany was the aggressor. By this time Mussolini's armies had already adopted the Nazi style of marching and Mussolini had passed racial laws against Jews within Italy, again copying Hitler. As Hitler's ally during the war, Mussolini was reduced to the role of Hitler's puppet and as the tide of the war turned against the Axis, Mussolini's support collapsed and he was overthrown in 1943. Installed as a puppet ruler in the north of Italy by his Nazi backers, he was eventually captured by partisans, executed, and his corpse was hung upside down from a petrol station and disfigured by an angry mob. It was in order to avoid a similar fate that Hitler left instructions that after his suicide his body should be reduced to ashes.

And yet even at this point distinctions can be drawn between the foreign policy of the two dictators. Essentially, Hitler was a fanatic, and Mussolini was an opportunist. As such, each man never took the other fully into his confidence. For example, Mussolini was not consulted regarding Germany's annexation of Austria, and Mussolini responded by annexing Albania without consulting or informing Germany. Therefore, despite Italy's "Pact of Steel" with Germany, Mussolini failed to join the war on Hitler's side at the outset, claiming that Italy was militarily unprepared for the conflict. This was quite true, but not the whole story. Ciano, Mussolini's foreign minister, had met with Hitler in August 1939 and expressed alarm about the escalating crisis between Germany and Poland. Hitler offered reassurances that this would remain a "localised war", but Ciano remained unconvinced, confiding to his diary that "I am certain that even if the Germans were given more than they ask for they would attack just the same, because they are possessed by the demon of destruction". Days later, Mussolini sent Hitler a telegram making it clear that Italy would remain neutral in any war between Germany and Poland.

In the final count, the foreign policy of both Hitler and Mussolini was ultimately and undoubtedly a failure: they had aimed for prestige and power for their countries, yet brought instead humiliation and destruction. Nevertheless, up until the mid-1930s it was Mussolini alone among the statesman of Europe who had the foresight and the strength to stand up to the threat of Nazism. In this light, his unholy alliance with Nazi Germany from 1936 onwards can be seen as the result not of admiration for Hitler or even of a cynical desire to get glory on the cheap, but rather of desperation and despair at the refusal of France and Britain to stand up to Hitler. In this respect, Fascist Italy found itself in much the same position as Soviet Russia in the years leading up to 1939. Mussolini had planned to "bleat with the sheep and howl with the wolves": he ended up bleating with the wolves and howling at the sheep, stating that "If Britain wins, we lose; if Germany wins, we are lost". By this time, Mussolini's foreign policy was not merely unsuccessful; it was not even Mussolini's: a fact he recognized when he described himself in a 1945 interview shortly before his death as "the last of the spectators".

Winston Churchill and German Emperor Wilhelm II during a military autumn manoeuvre near Breslau, Silesia, Germany in 1906.

9. WAS GERMANY TO BLAME FOR THE OUTBREAK OF BOTH WORLD WAR ONE AND WORLD WAR TWO IN EUROPE?

The superficial comparisons between the origins of World Wars One and Two are so numerous that the period 1914-45 has been referred to as "The European Civil War" (Enzo Traverso) and "The Second Thirty Years' War" (Sigmund Neumann). More specifically, historians such as Fritz Fischer have used the similarities between both wars to illustrate the fundamental continuity of a highly aggressive German foreign policy. Nevertheless, a closer examination highlights at least as many contrasts as comparisons, although this essay will seek to demonstrate that the primary cause of both wars was not Germany in particular but rather forces of nationalism in Europe as a whole.

The threat of a war on two fronts moulded German war plans before both wars. Formally declared as a sovereign state in the direct aftermath of the Franco-Prussian War of 1870-71, this was a state forged through the "Blood and Iron" policy of Chancellor Bismarck and which therefore regarded the military as the founding father of the nation. As a young, centralised, but largely landlocked country surrounded on all sides by potential enemies, she nurtured an aggressive strain of Prussian militarism and formulated uncompromising war plans. For example, before World War One Germany developed the notorious Schlieffen Plan, which operated on the basis of striking a pre-emptive blow against France – via neutral Belgium - before reeling the army around to attack Russia, who was regarded as the more serious threat. Similarly, Hitler's entire war strategy was based around neutralising Russia through the Nazi-Soviet Pact before unleashing Blitzkrieg against the West – a 'Lightning War' which took the view that general war against several enemies simultaneously was inevitable. In the view of Lewis Namier, "German desire to control Europe was the most important cause of both wars", although it is perhaps fairer to argue that before both wars Germany was trying to assert her position against the established empires of Britain and France.

Nevertheless, German war plans were the product of diplomatic desperation before World War One whereas they reflected cynical German ambition before World War Two. Before World War One, Germany perceived herself as a victim of an aggressive alliance system which had left her "encircled" by hostile powers. Germany was regarded as a parvenu upstart by the established powers of Russia, France and Britain following her creation at the end of the Franco-Prussian War in 1871. The alliance system developed by Chancellor Bismarck thereafter was specifically developed with the express intention of keeping Germany's enemies divided, and its breakdown in the 1890s after the retirement of Bismarck led to Germany's worst nightmare - the Franco-Russian Alliance (1894). This in turn was later consolidated by the entry of Britain in an arrangement that became known as the Triple Entente. The Kaiser attempted to break up the Triple Entente by exploiting tensions between Britain and France in the two Moroccan crises

(1905, 1911). However, this merely had the reverse effect of drawing them closer together to work against German ambitions and by 1914 a sense of fatalism had permeated the German military. However, in the years before World War Two, Germany's diplomatic position could not have been more different: Hitler was an absolute master of the diplomatic stage. The Western powers had recoiled from alliances altogether in favour of an ineffective policy of 'collective security' in the interwar period; they were also compromised by a sense of guilt that Germany had been treated badly in the peace treaties which followed World War One. As a result, Hitler repeatedly tricked them with such manoeuvres as the Anglo-German Naval Agreement (1935): this was a deliberate and successful ploy to draw Britain out of the Stresa Pact, which she had formed with Italy and France to keep Germany in check. Similarly, the remilitarisation of the Rhineland (March 1936), the Anschluss (March 1938) and the Sudeten Crisis (March-September 1938) were all presented by Hitler in terms of 'self-determination' rather than aggression.

In economic terms there are sharp distinctions between both origins of these wars - and once again Germany bears much less culpability for the outbreak of World War One than she does for World War Two. It is also notable that although Lenin (writing in *Imperialism: The Highest Stage of Capitalism*) argued that World War One was caused by economic factors, this is truer in fact for the second conflict. Admittedly, Fritz Fischer claimed to spot a *Sonderweg* (Special Path) of German history – namely, an obsession with seizing neighbouring territory as a prerequisite for national development. However, this view is not entirely convincing. Although in retrospect Bethmann-Hollwegg's September Programme (1914) and the punitive Treaty of Brest Litovsk (1918) suggests a Germany bent on stripping vast territory away from neighbours in Europe, these can be seen as the direct result of the pressures of war, not as the causes of it. Before 1914, the Kaiser actually talked almost exclusively in terms of African Colonies ("a place in the sun") when discussing German territorial ambitions – colonies that he saw primarily as a matter of prestige and power politics rather than of genuine economic value.

However, Hitler's Germany was operating against the backdrop of the Great Depression and so focused its attention much more covetously on resource-rich lands in the East. The importance of *Lebensraum* (living space) and resources from Eastern Europe was stated explicitly by Hitler in *Mein Kampf*, and were later reinforced in the Hossbach Memorandum (1937) and the seizure of the Sudetenland. The Nazi "economic miracle" which saw unemployment all but evaporate came at the expense of committing Germany to a war economy: loans were raised to finance re-armament, but these could only be repaid if these newly manufactured weapons were used to seize foreign lands and resources. In particular, the Four-Year Plan (1936) accelerated the pace of re-armament and had the express objective of making Germany ready for war within four years. In this respect AJP Taylor was quite correct when he said that "No matter what political reasons are given for war, the underlying reason is always economic".

Even on the broadest issues of ideology, there remain sharp distinctions between both wars. The dominant ideology that caused World War One was nationalism, with its abhorrent insistence on neighbours being not only different, but inferior. Whether the Kaiser's belief that all German-speaking peoples should unite (Pan-Germanism), the Russian concept that Slavic people should do the same (Pan-Slavism), or US President Woodrow Wilson's idea that all national minorities should be free to decide upon the futures through plebiscites (self-determination, later used by Hitler to justify the expansion of the Third Reich into sovereign states like Austria, Czechoslovakia and Poland), the period before World War One was characterised by a rampant patriotism that bordered on xenophobia.

However, in the years after World War One there was not just one, but several dominant ideologies that were radicalised and fragmented. The Western democracies superficially abandoned nationalistic flag-waving in favour of a Wilsonian policy of 'collective security' through the League of Nations; the Germans turned towards Nazi ideology, which took the doctrine of ultra-nationalism and took it to its logical conclusion of extreme racism; and the Russians had gone communist. In essence, the democracies pursued a policy of appeasement, fatally and exactly at the same time that the insanity of 'Aryan Supremacy' seized control of Hitler's Germany. This brings us to a final interesting point of contrast between the two wars: the first war was partly a product of ignorance on all sides about the attendant horrors of industrialised warfare, whereas the second was a product of the democracies being all too aware of those horrors and desperately seeking to avoid them even if it meant giving in to Hitler's demands and thereby making him even stronger. Ultimately, following Hitler's invasion of Czechoslovakia in March 1939 they chose to risk economic bankruptcy by gearing for war rather than acknowledging moral bankruptcy by continuing to avoid it.

In essence, both World War One and World War Two were the result to some extent of Germany's aggressive military strategies. However, Germany was much more a victim of diplomatic and economic forces before World War One than she was before World War Two. In any case, the question of Germany's responsibility is, in the final analysis, irrelevant: both wars were caused primarily by poisonous forces of nationalism, which bred unhealthy competition, xenophobia, paranoia and ultimately racism. World War One stemmed immediately from rampant patriotism on all sides and an ignorance that the horrors of industrialised warfare would create. World War Two stemmed immediately from a still more rampant Nazi hatred of other races fatally matched by the unwillingness of the democracies to face up to their responsibilities. The reason why the second half of the twentieth century in Europe had no more generalised conflicts on this scale is because finally all nations recognised the dehumanising brutality of war, and worked together to eradicate the economic and political divisions between sovereign states that had so frequently led to conflict in the period 1914-45.

Detail from a Chinese postage stamp, 1950, showing Joseph Stalin and Mao Zedong shaking hands.

10. HOW SIMILAR WAS THE RISE TO POWER OF STALIN AND MAO?

At first glance, the rise to power of Stalin and Mao appear easily comparable: both were members of deeply divided communist parties, and both operated within societies that suffered from civil war and the ever-present threat of foreign attack. Moreover, both the USSR and China were mainly populated by a disaffected peasantry - despite the fact that Karl Marx, the founding father of communism, had developed his theories around the principle that the first successful revolutions would take place in countries with an educated, industrialised proletariat.

Despite this, there are some challenges for the historian adopting a comparative approach. For example, Stalin's challenge was rising to power within a party which was already in government. By the time that Lenin died in 1924 and Stalin began his bid for power in earnest, the Bolshevik government was already more than six years old. In marked contrast, at exactly the same time Mao was fighting not just to gain leadership of the Chinese Communist Party (CCP), but also to bring it to power in the country as a whole – a battle which would take a further 25 years of instability characterised not only by Japanese invasion and occupation but also civil war against his nationalist rivals, Chiang Kai-Shek's Kuomintang (KMT).

Moreover, as communists both men were ideologically expected to believe in collective government, not personal dictatorship, so it is difficult to pinpoint exactly when each became the undisputed leader of their parties. For sake of simplicity, this essay will regard Stalin's announcement of the first Five Year Plan (1928) as signalling his emergence as *de facto* leader of the Bolshevik Party, whilst Mao's defining moment is his formal appointment as Chairman of the victorious Communist Party at the end of the Chinese Civil War (1949).

Although Stalin was already a member of a party in power by the time of Lenin's death, the regime was by no means secure within the country as a whole. Like Mao, he therefore placed great emphasis on the relationship of the regime with the peasantry, who formed the majority of the population in both countries and whose agriculture provided the bedrock of their economies. Nevertheless, although they shared this same concern, they addressed it in completely different ways.

Stalin's attitude towards the peasantry was almost unremittingly confrontational. In line with his Bolshevik beliefs, Stalin was hostile to the idea of mass movements in general and those relying upon peasant support in particular, which can be illustrated by two examples. First, in 1921 he persuaded the Politburo to send Red Army troops into his homeland of Georgia; he then used intimidation and physical violence against local officials, alarming even Lenin, whose "Final Testament" called for Stalin's influence within the party to be drastically curtailed. Secondly, after a period of tactically supporting a more moderate line against the peasants, in 1928 Stalin announced his first Five-Year Plan in terms of a war on the peasantry, a 'revolution from above' characterised by rapid industrialisation financed by compulsory requisitioning of grain. Peasant resistance to this ultimately resulted in an even more confrontational policy of forced collectivisation and the declaration that his objective was to deal the peasantry "such a blow that it will no longer rise to its feet".

In marked contrast to Stalin, and in exactly the same year that the Five-Year Plans were announced, Mao defined himself as the ally rather than as the enemy of the peasantry. Unlike Stalin, as a young revolutionary he completely disagreed with the Bolshevik view that the proletariat was the key to communist revolution, arguing that "The peasants are the sea. We are the fish. The sea is our habitat". Mao put his beliefs into practice following the attack of the communists by Nationalist forces in the "White Terror" of 1927. Fleeing to the agricultural province of Jiangxi, he proceeded to forge strong links with its 3 million peasants, who, in the words of the Red Army General Peng Dehuai, "dug up from the ground the grain which they had hidden from the KMT troops and gave it to us". At the same time that Stalin was engaged in a policy of violent requisitioning and confiscation against the peasantry of the Soviet Union, the peasants of China welcomed Mao's peasant-based revolutionary programme and responded enthusiastically to the declaration of the short-lived "Socialist Republic" in 1931.

Surrounded by hostile forces, the communists were ultimately forced to abandon Jiangxi in the famous "Long March" to Yenan (1934-1935), but Mao used this experience to "sow seeds" among the peasant communities he encountered during the 6000-mile trek ("Learn from the masses, and then teach them"). After establishing the "Yenan Soviet", the Chinese

Communist Party (CCP) continued to gain the support of the local populations by treating them with consideration. His soldiers were educated to use persuasion, not force, to win the hearts and minds of the peasantry. The "Eight Rules" of the Red Army meant that Mao's communists respected women, paid for crops, and ran literacy classes. The American journalist Edgar Snow, who visited Mao during this period, observed that "All forms of taxation were abolished ... to give the farmers a breathing-space. Second, the Reds gave land to the land-hungry peasants ... However, both the landlord and the rich peasant were allowed as much land as they could till with their own labour". The contrast with Stalin could not be more glaring.

With regard to Stalin, the Bolshevik Party in the USSR was deeply divided by the time of Lenin's death over policy towards the peasantry, and throughout this period, Stalin refrained from making public statements on the issue in order to maximise his freedom of manoeuvre. In 1921, Lenin decided to abandon the policy of "War Communism", which he now characterised as a "temporary measure" to which he had been "forced to resort to by extreme want, ruin and war". In place of compulsory requisitioning came a proportional tax to provide peasants with more incentive to produce grain. The partial revival of capitalism in this New Economic Policy (NEP) was highly controversial. The right-wing of the party, led by Bukharin, vigorously defended gradual, peasant-based socialism and encouraged the peasants to "enrich yourselves through the NEP". The Left Communists, however, felt that more emphasis needed to be placed on a programme of massive and rapid industrialisation if the regime was to survive. Represented most powerfully by Trotsky and his "Platform of 46", they described the NEP as "the first sign of the degeneration of Bolshevism".

China's CCP was equally divided about the role of the peasantry. However, in contrast to Stalin, Mao's strategy was not to adopt a "wait and see" approach, but to take a very bold and active part in these debates, leading a wing of the party which campaigned tirelessly for a peasant-based revolution. The success of his social programmes in Jiangxi – which he pursued without waiting for official sanction from party headquarters in Shanghai - allowed Mao to rapidly rise to a position of political pre-eminence within the CCP. This process was considerably aided when, in 1930, the party adopted the "Li Lisan Line", named after its new party chairman. This promoted the idea of a Bolshevik-style revolution in China spearheaded by the industrial proletariat and led by a centralised party elite. However, the incipient uprisings were crushed by the Nationalist forces of Chiang Kai-Shek, and Li Lisan was deposed the following year on the orders of the "28 Bolsheviks" – a group of young Chinese Communists trained by, and acting on the orders of, the Soviet Union. Mao had firmly opposed the "Li Lisan Line", arguing that "If we allot ten points to the revolution…seven points must go to the peasants", and thereby his reputation within the party was considerably enhanced.

The party divisions shared by Mao and Stalin were compounded by sharply contrasting military conditions. In military terms, Stalin's position was superficially weak. On the one hand, his main rival in the party, Leon Trotsky, enjoyed an impressive reputation. After successfully masterminding the strategy for the seizure of power in October 1917, Trotsky had been appointed Commissar for War. In this role, he built up the Red Army into a formidable fighting force that ensured Bolshevik victory in the Civil War (1918-1920). In contrast, Stalin's own war record was unimpressive. During the Civil War, whilst serving as Commissar to Tsaritsyn, Stalin had obstructed Trotsky's "military experts" and even imprisoned them on a barge which then mysteriously sank. Stalin brushed aside Trotsky's objections by calling him an "operetta commander, a chatterbox", but although Lenin initially approved of this "ruthless" approach he soon became alarmed at his protégé's lack of judgement. In particular, Stalin disobeyed a direct order to support Tukhachevsky's push on Warsaw with a detachment of cavalry. Combined with his heavy-handed approach to the Georgian question outlined earlier, this contributed to Lenin's final recommendation that he be removed from office altogether.

Compared to Stalin, Mao's military position was much stronger, since his rivals in the party suffered defeats in battle that tarnished their reputations. In 1934, with Jiangxi under heavy siege by nationalist forces, the party leaders embarked on a complete evacuation of the province: the famous "Long March". However, by marching in a straight line, and lumbering themselves with massive amounts of inessential heavy equipment (such as typewriters), they became easy targets. In the Battle of Xiang, the KMT rounded on the communists and the Red Army lost 45,000 men – over 50% of their fighting force. In contrast, Mao himself had a highly developed sense of military strategy. He crushed an incipient rebellion in his ranks by massacring 3000 opponents in the Futien Incident of 1930, and continually stressed the importance of guerrilla warfare during the Jiangxi siege ("The guerrilla must move amongst the people as a fish swims in the sea"). This strategy was formally adopted by the CCP after the disaster at Xiang: the CCP forces broke into four armies, each of which adopted a twisting path which made predicting their location extremely difficult. During the Second Civil War (1946-49) Mao successfully appointed Lin Biao as his military commander, which contributed to the final triumph over the KMT in the "Three Great Campaigns".

Although their reaction to these situations was very different, both Stalin and Mao proved remarkably adept at turning them to fullest advantage. Stalin astutely realised that Trotsky's very success was a source of great unease within the party. Stressing Lenin's expressed desire for a "collective leadership" after his death, and playing on his own reputation as a "grey blur" (Sukhanov), Stalin initially capitalised on divisions in the Left-Wing of the party. Kamenev and Zinoviev were persuaded to ally with Stalin against Trotsky, who they feared was showing dictatorial ("Bonapartist") tendencies as Red Army chief. Once Trotsky had been expelled from the Politburo, Stalin cynically allied himself with Bukharin and other right-wingers to expel Kamenev and Zinoviev. In late 1927, Stalin then turned against Bukharin and rejected the NEP in favour of agricultural collectivisation and massive industrialisation. Bukharin secretly attempted to form an alliance with Kamenev and Zinoviev, arguing that unless he was ousted Stalin would eventually destroy the communist revolution ("[Stalin is] an unprincipled intriguer who subordinates everything to his appetite for power"). Nevertheless, by this time Stalin had appointed so many supporters to senior positions in the party that his position was unassailable. In 1929 Bukharin was expelled from the Politburo.

Mao too deftly turned the ideological and military divisions within his party to full advantage with a series of well-timed manoeuvres, although characteristically he did this through the force of his personality and achievements rather than by manipulating factions and working in the shadows. For example, during the Long March in 1935, Mao spoke out boldly at the Tsunyi Conference, blaming the party's recent misfortunes on some of those out-of-touch "28 Bolsheviks". The vote which followed saw the triumvirate of Bo Gu, Otto Braun and Zhou Enlai demoted to different degrees. Braun later reflected that this represented a total victory for Mao, "thereby subordinating the party itself to his will". However, Mao himself wisely refrained from making a bid for complete power at this point, later recalling that at the Tsunyi conference "some people would have had me as the core, but I would have nothing of the kind". Only slowly did a cult of personality develop around Mao ("The Great Helmsman"), although by 1945 a Central Committee Resolution claimed that "The Tsunyi Meeting...inaugurated a new central leadership, headed by Comrade Mao - a historic change of paramount importance in the Chinese Communist Party".

Although domestic factors played a central role, there was also an international dimension to the rise to power of both dictators. Both Mao and Stalin benefitted from a sense of affronted nationalism and fear of foreign influence which allowed these communists to perversely present themselves as patriotic defenders of their homelands. However, whereas the danger to Soviet Russia was largely theoretical by the time that Stalin came to power, China had suffered for decades from direct and devastating foreign intervention by the time that Mao took control. As a result, Stalin had to actively stoke the flames of nationalist fervour in a way that Mao never found necessary.

Western colonialism had led to China's major trade and ports being under foreign control as early as the turn of the 20th century. Despite fighting on the side of the Allies during World War One, China's claims for self-determination had been ignored by the Big Three at Versailles, who instead gave Germany's base in China (Shandong) to Japan. The immediate beneficiary of this tide of offended nationalism – as to be expected – was the Nationalist KMT party, who – with the support of the CCP - launched the "Northern March" against the Warlords and their imperialist backers in 1923. However, when Chiang Kai-Shek became leader of the party, he squandered this support by rounding on his former allies in the CCP and becoming obsessed with their destruction even after the Japanese invaded Manchuria in 1931. Chiang Kai-Shek's insistence on attacking, rather than uniting, with the CCP against the Japanese was highly unpopular, and his increasing reliance upon American aid tainted the KMT with the reputation of being in the pocket of foreign colonialists. By 1945, the KMT armies had lost their most experienced officers, the political leadership was divided and the economy was suffering from rampant hyperinflation. It was in these circumstances that Mao was able to advance on Beijing and declare the Communist Republic of China on October 1st, 1949.

Stalin made a deliberate point of capitalising upon his people's fears of foreign exploitation and invasion. These anxieties were by no means unfounded, because Soviet Russia had become a pariah state after World War One. Its decision to pull out of the war, renounce Tsarist war debts and campaign for a world revolution precipitated foreign intervention in the ensuing civil war. Britain, France, Japan and the United States all invaded the Soviet Union in the belief that communism should, in the words of Churchill, be "strangled in its cradle". Denied entry to the League of Nations (which Trotsky denounced in any case as "an organization for the bloody suppression of the toilers"), the Soviet Union had signed the Rapallo Treaty with her fellow international outcast, Germany, in 1922. Nevertheless, Germany was rapidly re-integrated into the international community through the Dawes Plan (1924) and the Locarno Treaties (1925). In 1926, Germany joined the League, the former white general Pilsudski seized Poland, and the USSR's sense of isolation and vulnerability was complete.

However, whilst these anxieties were real, the threat of an actual foreign invasion by the late 1920s was minimal. Stalin therefore went to great lengths to generate a "War Scare" through which he could finally step out of the shadows with his own radicalised brand of Marxism. He "fostered and exploited fear of foreign attack" (Susan Sontag), giving mass publicity to the 1928 Shakhty trial when 55 engineers in Donbass were found guilty of industrial espionage for the West on trumped-up charges (five were executed). He cleverly appealed to a sense of outraged nationalism by discarding Trotsky's pursuit of "World Revolution" in favour of "Socialism in One Country" and depicting his new Five-Year Plans for industry and agriculture as an act of patriotic necessity: "We are 50 or 100 years behind the advanced countries. We must make good this lag in 10 years. Either we do it, or they crush us." With this speech Stalin finally emerged as a theorist in his own right and the undisputed leader of the Soviet Union.

Essentially, the conditions faced by Stalin and Mao were broadly similar, but the methods they adopted towards these issues could not have been more different. Stalin viciously attacked the peasantry whereas Mao enthusiastically embraced them. Stalin exploited fears about the military ambitions of his rivals, whereas Mao instead capitalized upon his own abilities in the arts of war. Stalin owed his initial rise within the party to his apparent lack of ideological conviction, whereas Mao owed his ascendancy to bold and uncompromising ideological pronouncements. Yet in their manipulation of the international situation, Stalin spoke with strident passion, whereas Mao adopted an altogether more passive approach. Of all these contrasts, the most significant is surely the fact that Mao saw the mass of the people he sought to rule as allies rather than enemies: a fact which helps to explain why the USSR ultimately imploded, whereas China remains not merely in the hands of a communist government, but appears destined to become one of the superpowers of the 21st century.

Joseph Stalin, Secretary-general of the Communist party of the Soviet Union, c.1939

11. TO WHAT EXTENT DID STALIN ACHIEVE HIS OBJECTIVES AS RULER OF THE SOVIET UNION BY 1941?

Stalin's immediate objectives upon securing power in the Soviet Union were economic. He stated in 1928 at the launch of the first Five Year Plan "to convert the USSR from an agrarian and weak country…independent of world capitalism". Through a policy of collectivisation in the countryside and mass industrialisation in the cities, he aimed to protect the USSR from what he regarded as the inevitable military showdown with the capitalist West. However, the initial dislocation and distress caused by Stalin's "Great Turn" threatened his political survival. The wave of terror which he unleashed successfully transformed Stalin into a totalitarian dictator with a burgeoning cult of personality; nevertheless, these personal triumphs were at the expense of his ideological convictions and his historical reputation.

In agriculture, Stalin's policy of collectivisation was adopted not merely in order to improve productivity through economies of scale. Important though this was to provide the necessary sustenance for the industrial workers, there were other potential benefits to this policy. Its success would, for example, isolate the Bukharin faction on the right of the Communist Party by demonstrating a viable alternative to the capitalist concessions of the New Economic Policy (NEP) that retained elements of capitalism. Moreover, the anticipated (arguably even hoped-for) resistance of the wealthier peasants would have the effect of creating an ideological showdown with the capitalist kulak peasant class in general and with the Ukrainian nationalists in particular.

In some respects, and against these criteria, Stalin's policies were clearly successful. The comprehensive rejection of the NEP left Bukharin and his allies isolated and Stalin's political position superficially strengthened. By 1941, virtually all farming had been collectivized and 17 million peasants were freed up to work in factories. All Soviet farmers belonged to collectivised farms (*Kolkhoz*) or newly created state farms (*Sovkhoz*).

Nevertheless, although ideologically sound, the resistance of the most talented and successful kulak peasant farmers to the policy of collectivisation was economically and socially ruinous. In the words of Alan Shukman, "What began as an economic policy quickly turned the countryside into a scene of despair, bloodshed and terror". The most infamous result was the Ukrainian famine, or *Holodomor,* which killed perhaps 8 million people. It remains hotly debated whether Stalin deliberately engineered this famine; in 2008, the Ukrainian Parliament voted that Stalin's collectivisation policies were a deliberate act of "genocide", with Moscow angrily retorting that this was "unilaterally rewriting history" in order to strengthen anti-Russian feeling. Whatever the truth of the matter, it is clear that Stalin did little to alleviate the famine and indeed exacerbated the crisis by continuing to export grain rather than use it for hunger relief. Production in all fields of agriculture collapsed during the first Five-Year Plan to such an extent that Stalin was humiliatingly forced to temporarily halt the programme in 1930, claiming that the pace of change needed to be reduced as the party had become "Dizzy with Success". Thereafter, production levels crept upwards but these did not reach their pre-1928 levels again until 1953, the year of Stalin's death.

In industry, Stalin's policy of mass industrialisation and state control were motivated by similarly multifarious aims. As well as creating a strong, modern economy, his policy would help to create more proletarians for the socialist motherland; it was a perverse fact that the first communist revolution took place in a country which remained primarily agricultural - as Trotsky had noted, "there is not enough proletarian yeast in our peasant dough".

Stalin's policy was clearly successful in some respects. Women were encouraged into the workforce by being provided with a generous childcare provision, and showpiece projects were created such as the Dneiper Dam and the Magnitogorsk power station. Within the first five years Russian industry at least doubled its output when Europe was suffering from the Great Depression; it was at this time that the international kudos of communism reached its zenith. Through the Five-Year Plans, Stalin was able to build vast new industrial centres to the East of the Ural Mountains and so away from Soviet Union's vulnerable Western borders. This helped to ensure that the Soviet economy did not completely collapse following the Nazi invasion of 1941.

However, the policy was not without its failures. In economic terms, the emphasis was on quantity of production, not quality; therefore many machines broke down and production lines were held up by supply bottlenecks, although these problems were invariably blamed on "saboteurs" and "wreckers".

Therefore, although many workers felt they were taking part in a grand socialist experiment, many others were subject to intimidation in the form of production targets for every worker and terror as in the 1928 Shakhty Trial against Western 'spies'. The most unfortunate were reduced to the status of slave labourers. The camp system, the Gulag, was populated by prisoners provided from arrest quotas in order to provide workers for the largest Soviet projects such as the Belomor Canal which led to the death of an estimated 100,000 workers. Many of these camps were located in the coldest regions of Siberia, where winter temperatures fell as low as minus 50 degrees Celsius. Disturbing from an ideological perspective was the way in which Stalin abandoned his communist principles in pursuit of short-term economic gain such as using the US-capitalist corporation Ford to build factories, and adopting the Stakhanovite programme, which shamelessly rewarded the most productive workers with perks and wage bonuses. Overall, Stalin's economic policies saw the USSR veer wildly away from any compromise with capitalism in the countryside in a desperate attempt to discredit the NEP, whilst shamelessly adopting capitalist practices in industry despite the inherent contradictions in doing so.

The socio-economic chaos caused by the "Great Turn" towards collectivisation and industrialization seriously jeopardised Stalin's political ascendancy within the Bolshevik Party. The discovery of the Ryutin Platform (1932), a 200-page document which called for Stalin's removal as General Secretary on the basis of his "ungovernable adventurism" in economic policy, was all the more disconcerting given how difficult it was for Stalin to determine exactly how many people supported it. Stalin's sense of insecurity was heightened by the rapturous reception given to Sergei Kirov when he delivered a speech critical of collectivisation at the Seventeenth Party Congress.

Kirov was assassinated in mysterious circumstances shortly afterwards. It is impossible to know for sure whether Stalin ordered this assassination or was genuinely shocked by it, but either way he capitalised on the event by ordering a series of Show Trials which were used to clear the party of his enemies, both perceived and real. By 1938 all of his old rivals - Kamenev, Zinoviev, Bukharin, Rykov, Tomsky - were dead. Moreover, 1,108 of the 1,966 delegates to the Seventeenth "Congress of the Condemned" were later purged.

Although this meant that in a narrow political sense Stalin's position was now unassailable, the momentum of the Purges in the party now spread uncontrollably into the country as a whole, with profoundly damaging results for the USSR, and for the reputation of communism up to this day. For whilst it is true that the Bolshevik Party had never shied away from violence as a tool of political control – the "Red Terror" of the Civil War period being a case in point – Lenin had used violence as a tool of brutal expediency and against clearly defined enemies of socialism. Stalin, however, turned it into a fundamental feature of the Soviet state and used it not only against some of the most respected members of his own party, but also indiscriminately against innocent Soviet citizens. The period of "The Terror" – sometimes known as the *Yezhovschina* after the NKVD chief who presided over its worst excesses – saw hundreds of thousands of Soviet citizens tortured and executed on hearsay evidence or deported to the Gulag. Militarily, the execution of Marshall Tukhachevsky and the purging of a further 35,000 army officers crippled the armed forces and is considered one of the major reasons for the spectacular Nazi successes in the early months of the German invasion of the Soviet Union in 1941.

Whilst the economic policies of collectivisation and industrialisation drastically increased the role of the state, the Purges and the Terror centralised power within the hands of

Stalin himself, thereby creating a cult of personality. Arguably, and somewhat surprisingly, it is in this area of cultural and social policy that Stalin had the most success and generated the most genuine support. During the Great Depression, Western writers and journalists flocked to see for themselves the economic progress being secured by the Five-Year Plans, including HG Wells, George Bernard Shaw and the cartoonist David Low. The First Congress of Soviet Writers (1934) called upon authors to "Show Stalin in all his magnitude" and this produced such embarrassing nonsense as the poetry of Avdienko ("When the woman I love presents me with a child the first word it shall utter will be: Stalin").

This cult of personality was later explicitly condemned by Khrushchev as being fundamentally against the spirit of socialism, but the reality was that Engels had acknowledged that this was with "the exception of cases when it had an important purpose". Moreover, even Marx stated that the socialist phase which would come between capitalism and communism would be characterised by a centralisation of authority as the foundations for the future workers' paradise were laid. Therefore, in ideological terms the principle of Stalin's cult of personality could be rationalised and justified.

In terms of social policies, it has to be acknowledged that this propaganda was based on some genuine successes. In educational terms, Stalin placed great emphasis on vocational qualifications, setting up the *RABFACs* (Technical Colleges) to serve this purpose. Stalin also focused on academic training; he re-introduced examinations which tested literacy skills in particular. This policy resulted in the literacy rate leaping from almost nothing to 86% in rural areas. Women were encouraged to enter the workforce and were given child allowances, health clubs and childcare facilities. Factory workers were entitled to an annual holiday, and health care was also expanded; for the first time, the poorer people of Russia could expect qualified medical help in times of illness. This is not to say that Stalin's policies were totally successful - in Moscow, only 6% of households had more than one room, for example - but they do suggest that the basis of Stalin's power was at least partly due to positive support.

Stalin was clearly successful in his objective of modernising Russia through a drastic policy of collectivisation and industrialisation. In this way he was able to ensure that if or when war developed to threaten the USSR, the state was sufficiently robust to prevent the country's collapse. Nevertheless, in a military sense Stalin's purges of his most talented soldiers in the years immediately prior to the 1941 invasion by Germany meant that the Soviet Union's victory was by no means assured. The social and political cost of his policies was also immense. Notwithstanding the various improvements that took place under his regime which helped to solidify his cult of personality, the Purges and the Terror were directly necessitated by Stalin's need to target scapegoats for the failure of his economic policies and to provide slave labour for his most ambitious industrial projects. Stalin had created a country whose citizens and leaders lived in a permanent state of fear and suspicion – much like Stalin himself, who in a rare unguarded moment shortly before his death in 1953 admitted that "I trust no one, not even myself".

Allied Occupation Zones of Germany after World War Two

12. FOR WHAT REASONS, AND WITH WHAT RESULTS, WAS GERMANY A SOURCE OF COLD WAR TENSION BETWEEN 1945 AND 1962?

"Berlin is the testicles of the West. Every time I want the West to scream, I squeeze on Berlin". Khrushchev's characteristically earthy metaphor reminds us that Germany was a source of Cold War tension for a number of important reasons in the period 1945-1962. This essay will consider three illustrative examples in particular: the initial debates about the status of Germany after World War Two; the Berlin Blockade of 1948-1949; and the final crisis of 1961-62 which culminated in the building of the Berlin Wall. The reasons for each of these crises will be outlined in this essay with an essential narrative of events, whilst the results will be considered in a more analytical perspective. In this way it will be demonstrated that Germany was a source of tension for so many years because, as Soviet foreign minister Molotov put it, "What happens to Berlin, happens to Germany; what happens to Germany, happens to Europe".

One reason why Germany was a source of Cold War tension stems from the fact that the wartime allies were unable to reach a satisfactory conclusion about how the country should be partitioned between them at the end of World War Two. At the Yalta and Potsdam conferences there was tortuous debate on this issue which culminated in the decision that Germany would be split into four zones (British, French, Soviet, American). Berlin, the capital city, would also be divided into four zones. The French zones of Germany, on the insistence of Stalin, were carved out of the British and American sectors. Germany would pay reparations, but there were debates about the actual amount and form these would take (a commission was therefore appointed to look into the matter). The Allies also agreed to bring Nazi war criminals to justice and the Germans would be subjected to a period of "Denazification". A "Committee on Dismemberment of Germany" was set up, with its purpose being to decide how Germany was to be divided. Reversion of all German annexations in Europe, including the Sudetenland, Alsace-Lorraine, Austria, and the westernmost parts of Poland was also agreed. By the time of the Potsdam Conference the Soviets had taken control of Berlin and Germany had surrendered. The zones of Germany were finalized, and armies of occupation moved into them; Berlin, deep in the Soviet zone, was divided in the same way. Stalin agreed at Potsdam that the Western Allies should have access to road, rail and air routes to reach their zones of Berlin.

The ultimate results of these pragmatic but rather impractical agreements were further tensions. Germany's Eastern border was shifted West to the Oder-Neisse line, reducing Germany's size by 25% to compensate Poland for lands lost to the USSR and creating a wave of 500,000 German refugees. The lack of agreement over reparations meant that the USSR continued to strip its sector of Germany of raw materials, machinery and even slave labour, with Stalin justifying this, not unfairly, as war reparations since the war cost the Soviet Union 27 million lives - 40 times more than American and British losses put together.

The practicality of having Western zones of Berlin deep within East Germany was likely to cause tensions in the future. Even the Nuremberg trials of German war criminals became a source of contention; Stalin came to see them as too lenient (he was particularly scathing of "Operation Paperclip", which saw Nazi weapons scientists like Wernher von Braun spirited away to work on the US missile programme rather than put on trial) and the West increasingly grew sensitive to claims that they were mere 'victor's justice'; Hermann Goering, the highest ranking surviving Nazi at the trials, stated with some justification that had the Nazis won, Churchill would have been put on trial for the firebombing of Dresden and Truman for dropping atomic bombs on Japan.

After the wartime conferences and their aftermath, the next reason why Germany became a source of Cold War tension can be understood through reference to the Berlin Blockade. The cause of this crisis was that the agreements reached at Yalta and Potsdam about Germany were, in practice, untenable. In particular, the status of the Western zones of Berlin as a capitalist island in a communist sea was a source of immense irritation and embarrassment for Stalin; whilst the West poured Marshall Aid into the Western zones in a major process of reconstruction, the USSR continued to strip its zones of Germany and Berlin of resources, with the result that a gaping discrepancy emerged between conditions in the two areas. It was against this background that the UK and USA unilaterally decided to merge their zones of Germany into one united area called 'Bizonia' which formed the nucleus of a new West German State with its own currency, the Deutschmark. Stalin was not consulted about this in advance and was understandably outraged.

The immediate result was that Stalin blockaded all rail and road routes into Berlin – more out of desperation than aggression, an attempt to force the West back to the negotiating table than out of any desire for 'world revolution'. The commander of the American occupation zone in Germany, General Lucius Clay, wanted to send supplies into Berlin using an armed convoy of lorries. President Truman rejected this idea because he thought it could too easily lead to military confrontation, and instead authorised the Berlin Airlift – gambling that Stalin would not escalate the conflict into another world conflict by shooting the planes down. At the lowest point of the blockade, West Berliners were living on dried potatoes, powdered eggs and cans of meat and had only 4 hours of electricity a day. The USA stationed B-29 bombers with the ability to carry atomic bombs, which the USSR did not have at this time, in Britain as an implicit message to Stalin, who tacitly admitted defeat by lifting the blockade in May 1949.

The deeper result of the Berlin Blockade was a hardening of Cold War barriers militarily, economically and politically. In 1949, the Western powers set up NATO (North Atlantic Treaty Organisation), declaring that an attack on any one of them would be considered an attack against them all. The Soviet Union ultimately reacted in 1955 with the Warsaw Pact – a military alliance of communist states. America, Britain and France also united their zones into the Federal Republic of Germany (West Germany). Stalin in turn set up the German Democratic Republic (East Germany) and continued to strip it of resources. In June 1953, workers in East Berlin rose in protest against their working conditions; within days, nearly a million East Germans had joined the protests, which were brutally crushed by Soviet tanks.

The third and final reason why Germany was a source of Cold War tensions can be analysed through a consideration of the Berlin Crisis of 1961. The immediate cause of this was the continuing "brain drain" of East Germans to the West through Berlin, leaving behind the harsh political climate and economic hardship of life under communism. Many of those who defected were educated or highly skilled workers and the East German authorities could not afford to lose their best and brightest citizens. Between 1949 and 1961, an estimated 2.7 million East Germans left for West Germany, and Berlin was the centre of this process as defectors had easy access to its Western sectors. At the Vienna Summit of 1961, Khrushchev (already alarmed by Kennedy's recent botched attempt to invade Cuba at the Bay of Pigs) therefore tried to persuade the US President to recognise the sovereignty of East Germany - which in turn would have nullified Allied rights in Berlin. He told Kennedy that "It's up to the US to decide whether there will be war or peace...The decision to sign a peace treaty [with East Germany] is firm and irrevocable". Kennedy responded: "Then, Mr. Chairman, there will be a war. It will be a cold winter". On Saturday August 12, 1961, East Berlin mayor Walter Ulbricht signed an order to close the border and erect a Wall. The tide of East Germans flooding to the West came to an abrupt end. Overnight, the door to freedom closed, and remained so until 1989.

The immediate result of the Berlin Crisis was that the Wall closed the biggest loophole in the Iron Curtain, and Berlin was transformed overnight from being one of the easiest places to cross from East Europe to West Europe to being one of the most difficult. The access checkpoints became an immediate point of contention: in October 1961, U.S. and Soviet tanks faced off against each other a mere 100 yards apart on either side of Checkpoint Charlie. General Clay was convinced that having US tanks use bulldozer mounts to knock down parts of the Wall would end the crisis to the greater advantage of the US and its allies without eliciting a Soviet military response. President Kennedy, however, refused to sanction such a policy, and over a period of months the Berlin Wall was rebuilt using concrete. Not only that, but buildings near the wall were demolished or incorporated into the wall itself to create a "death zone" in view of heavily armed East German guards.

In a diplomatic sense, the outcome of the Berlin Crisis of 1961 can therefore superficially be seen as undermining the prestige of the USA: Kennedy was wrong-footed by Khrushchev at the Vienna Summit and failed to react when the Berlin Wall was erected. Nevertheless, this is a superficial judgement of a delicate situation, and on balance Kennedy's handling of the Berlin crisis was pragmatic and firm. The building of the Wall was rightly seen by Kennedy as a sign that the Soviets no longer aimed to control the entire city of Berlin, and that this new rationalisation of the situation was preferable to conflict (as he put it, "a wall is a hell of a lot better than a war"). Although Khrushchev presented the wall as an "anti-fascist protection barrier", Kennedy realised that it was a terrible reflection on the communist system. When he delivered his famous "Ich bin ein Berliner" speech the following year, he stingingly observed that "Freedom has many difficulties and democracy is not perfect. But we have never had to put a wall up to keep our people in".

In the final analysis, the reasons why Germany was a source of Cold War tensions can be seen as stemming from the political significance of Germany as the fulcrum of the Nazi Reich, which made its status after World War Two an issue of contention between the Grand Alliance. The geographical position of Germany in the heart of Europe and the military dominance of the USSR in Berlin created further challenges which Yalta and Potsdam solved only in the short term and at the expense of an anomalous status for the city which triggered the Blockade of 1948-1949. This in turn hardened Cold War battle lines and set the scene for the final major crisis which culminated in the Berlin

Wall. Ironically, it was this ultimate human rights abuse which finally brought Cold War tensions over Germany to an end. The Soviets stopped the 'brain drain' out of Berlin, and the West were reassured that West Berlin was no longer under direct threat of occupation as a result. From this point forwards the Cold War would be fought not in Germany but in Eastern Europe and, more widely, in Asia.

War-weary Korean civilians pictured in June 1951

13. WHAT WERE THE CAUSES OF THE KOREAN WAR AND ITS CONSEQUENCES FOR THE KOREAS AND THE UNITED STATES?

The Korean War was one of the most significant conflicts of the 20th Century and the first clear indication that the Cold War would not be confined to Europe. When North Korean communist forces poured over the 38th Parallel into South Korea on 25th June 1950, US President Harry Truman mustered a UN force consisting of sixteen nations to come to the defence of the South. The initial success of US General MacArthur's audacious amphibious landing at Inchon was transformed into an international crisis when China threw 300,000 troops into the conflict, turning the tide and facilitating a truce along the lines where it had all started. Steven Denney argues that the Korean War can be seen as both a civil war between the two Koreas, and as an interstate war when the United States, acting through the UN, became involved. On this basis the causes and consequences of the war need to be assessed not just in domestic, but also in international terms.

The causes of the Korean War stem back to the tense division of the country along the 38th Parallel by the USSR and the USA at the end of World War Two. Although supposedly a temporary arrangement until national elections could be held, Cold War rivalry meant that by 1950 two rival governments had become entrenched: in the north, a communist regime under Kim Il Sung; in the south, a government established on more democratic lines under Syngman Rhee. Both these leaders can be held responsible for the conflict that followed. On the one hand, Rhee made aggressive statements to the effect that he planned to reunite the Korean peninsula under his leadership, using force if necessary. He had said to his adviser Dr. Robert Oliver that "North Korea should be recaptured by the force of arms…to fulfil the ancient nationality of Korea". On the other, Kim Il Sung used this as a justification to launch what Truman called a "sneak attack" by ordering his armies to attack over the 38th parallel in June 1950.

Nevertheless, like many Cold War conflicts, this was not merely a civil war with domestic causes, but an interstate war with superpower roots. For example, prior to Kim's invasion of the South in 1950, which triggered the Korean War, the USSR equipped his Korean People's Army (KPA) with modern, Soviet-built heavy tanks, trucks, artillery, and small arms. Kim also formed an air force. Kim explicitly sought the permission of Stalin before launching his attack; Stalin gave his blessing and a promise of 10-15,000 tons of oil in June and July on the understanding that the USSR would not get directly involved; "If you should get kicked in the teeth, I shall not lift a finger. You have to ask Mao for all the help". Thus Stalin had the power to avert the conflict, but chose not to do so. Similarly, on the other side of the ideological divide, President Truman was heavily criticised for pulling troops out of South Korea far too rapidly after World War Two after Secretary of State Dean Acheson announced that Korea lay outside the "defence perimeter" of the USA in Asia, with the result that the country was left dangerously weak and a tempting target for the KPA in the North. US Senator Taft noted that "our action in Korea itself invited attack. We withdrew our troops from Korea. We, in effect, said we're not going to engage in military operations".

As a war which started off as a civil conflict, and escalated into an international one, the consequences of the Korean War can be considered first in terms of Korea, then the United States. First of all, the immediate result for Korea was a loss of 4 million lives overall, from both Koreas. The Panmunjom armistice that ended the hostilities in 1953 was a truce rather than a peace treaty, and so Korea remains divided to this day: a million troops are massed either side of the 38th Parallel and conscription exists in both North and South Korea. In North Korea specifically, the initial result of the war was that the North became economically prosperous with the backing of the Soviet Union. However, as was the case with Castro's Cuba, this became an unhealthy dependence. As the Soviet economy collapsed in the 1990s, so did that of North Korea: a famine in the 1990s killed as much as 10% of the population. In stark contrast, South Korea, under the protection of the United States, entered into international trade agreements and received international investment, giving it one of the strongest economies in the world. South Korea's economy rapidly gained ground in the late 1960s, and the country now ranks as the fourth largest economy in Asia.

To turn to the USA, the immediate political implications of the Korean War were first of all disastrous for the Truman administration. By firstly encouraging MacArthur to invade North Korea after his successful landing at Inchon, then ordering a retreat back to the 38th Parallel when faced with the invasion of troops from China, Truman appeared to be snatching defeat from the jaws of victory. MacArthur openly criticised this policy and called for nuclear war against China if necessary, at which point Truman fired him. The President's popularity rating plummeted to 26% and he didn't even run for re-election, thereby ending almost 20 years of the Democratic Party's control of the White House. However, whilst the war weakened President Truman personally, it gave an alarming degree of power to the presidency. Truman had declared the war to be a mere "police action" and thereby avoided having to go through Congress to obtain a declaration of war. This set a dangerous military precedent: claiming their war-making authority rested in their power as Commanders-in-Chief, both Presidents Johnson and Nixon later refused to ask Congress for approval to wage war in and around Vietnam, a major factor in undermining support for that conflict. It was not until the Gulf War in 1991 that President Bush asked Congress for permission to wage war again.

Militarily too, the Korean War led to a fundamental rethink of US Cold War strategy. Eisenhower, keen to reassert American dominance in the fight against communism, adopted a policy of "massive retaliation" by threatening nuclear strikes against any further communist incursions (a policy which reached its terrifying climax during the Cuban Missile Crisis). This policy of brinkmanship was combined with a fresh round of alliances: two defence treaties were signed in 1951 with Japan and the Philippines. The same year the ANZUS Pact was signed between Australia, New Zealand and the United States, whilst in Indochina the United States increased aid to the French. Secondly, the USA established a chain of military bases around the world: in the words of Professor Charles Armstrong, "It was from the Korean War onward that we had a permanent, global American military presence that we had never had before. It was a real turning point for America's global role". As a result, the war led to an increase the power of what Eisenhower referred to as the "military-industrial complex": as David Goldfield states, "it confirmed the ideas behind NSC-68, with its call for US to expand its military and to lead an anti-communist alliance". Even today, the US remains committed to defending South Korea.

To summarize, the Korean War was a civil war caused partly by domestic factors, but these in turn were largely the product of superpower rivalries in the region. Hence, Korea experienced some disastrous socio-economic consequences in particular, but the United States suffered serious political and military fallout and in diplomatic terms the UN had to deal with increased superpower tension. Perhaps the most damaging result of the Korean War was how it twisted American foreign policy principles. The Truman doctrine had originally been based on the idea of protecting "free peoples" from the threat of "communist subversion". However, after the Korean War it was only anti-communism, rather than any commitment to freedom, which was required for a foreign regime to obtain American aid. This set the scene for US support not only for the despotic regime of Ngo Dinh Diem in South Vietnam, but also for dictators in Latin America including Batista in Cuba, Trujillo in the Dominican Republic, Papa Doc Duvalier in Haiti and Pinochet in Chile. It is on this basis that James Matray regards the "main legacy" of the Korean War as being that the "United States thereafter pursued a foreign policy of global intervention and paid an enormous price in death, destruction, and damaged reputation".

Jacobo Arbenz, pictured during his inauguration as President of Guatemala, 1951

14. IN WHAT WAYS, AND WITH WHAT RESULTS, DID THE COLD WAR INFLUENCE RELATIONS BETWEEN LATIN AMERICA AND THE UNITED STATES, 1945-1960?

The historical relationship between the USA and Latin America prior to 1945 was dominated by a patriarchal attitude moulded by concepts of Manifest Destiny and the Monroe Doctrine, each of which stressed the natural rights of the USA over other territories across and around the continent. The Cold War sharpened these attitudes but also changed them in some important respects. The main way in which the Cold War influenced relations between Latin America and the United States was to make US presidents much more uncompromising and even paranoid towards their neighbours. The result of this was to create further instability in the region and to irreparably damage the reputation of the United States as the leading democracy of the free world.

Ostensibly, the Cold War could have seen the United States adopt a more liberal attitude towards Latin America in the immediate aftermath of World War Two. After all, as Gaddis Smith explains, "The public rhetoric of American foreign policy, enshrined in the Truman Doctrine...proclaimed that democracy, freedom, the rights of the individual were the answer to Communism". This in turn built upon the "Good Neighbour" policy of President Franklin D. Roosevelt, which centred around non-intervention and non-interference in the domestic affairs of Latin America. However, three main figures in the new administration – President Truman, Dean Acheson and George Kennan – had an attitude towards Latin America which was patronising at best, racist at worst. Truman saw Latin Americans as "very emotional" and hard to work with, burdened with "a political culture too weak and selfish to ... resist the superior determination and skill of the Communist enemy". Secretary of State Dean Acheson similarly felt that Latin America's challenges were caused by a lack of "population control", "primitive politics, massive ignorance" and "archaic" societies. George Kennan, the founding architect of American Cold War policy, was sent on a fact-finding mission to Latin America in 1950 and returned to write a report in which he said that "extensive intermarriage" between Spaniards, "native people" and "Negro slave elements" had created a race of people suffering from "tremendous helplessness and impotence" masked with "exaggerated self-centeredness and egotism". With these views of Latin America, Truman's policies towards the region were hardened.

US policies were revised in the context of the early Cold War. In Bolivia, Truman adopted a policy of placing the containment of communism way above any respect for democracy. He withheld recognition from the left-leaning Bolivian government that came to power in the "National Revolution" of 1952. Eventually, the incumbent government, a right-wing, conservative autocracy, annulled the results. In 1952, the US National Security Council issued a secret document, NSC-141, which further prioritised diplomatic stability ahead of social justice. This reinforced the earlier Rio Treaty of 1947, which formalized the idea that an attack on one country in the Americas was an attack upon them all. It was clear to many that Latin American nations were now "compulsory, automatic allies of the United States" (Narciso García). This perception was reinforced at the Pan-American Conference in Bogota in 1948, which set up the Organization of American States (OAS), a collective security organization that was the continent's equivalent of NATO. After the "loss of China" in 1949 when the Republic of China fled to Taiwan and communists took over the rest of China, there was even less attention paid to improving social and economic conditions in Latin America: instead, Truman announced his "Point Four Program", which focused on providing technical aid to Asia and Africa. In protest, Louis Joseph Halle of the Policy Planning Staff at the State Department wrote an anonymous article in 1950 for Foreign Affairs magazine as 'Mr Y', condemning the lack of economic support for Latin America.

President Eisenhower came to power in 1952 obsessed, as had been Truman, with the Soviet Union. He promised a "New Look" in foreign affairs characterised by the aggressive 'rollback' of the communist threat. As a result, any US policy innovation that was pursued in Latin America was to the detriment of the countries concerned. Eisenhower continued Truman's policy of preventing communism from gaining a foothold even if this was at the expense of social justice. His method was not to fund developmental aid or vigorously promote political democracy; on the contrary, he supported anti-communist, non-democratic governments throughout the region regardless of human rights abuses. By 1954, Latin America had 13 dictators among its 20 states. When there were demands for the State Department to protest on behalf of the political prisoners held in the dungeons of the dictator Pérez

Jiménez of Venezuela, US Secretary of State Dulles refused. President Eisenhower awarded a Legion of Merit to the dictator of Peru, Manuel Odría, in a grand ceremony, offering congratulations for his "energy and firmness of purpose" regarding the "problem of Communist infiltration".

The results of Eisenhower's policies for Latin American countries were damaging. For example, Eisenhower reacted aggressively when Guatemala elected the social reformer Jacobo Arbenz as president in 1951 in the country's first ever peaceful transition of power. Arbenz launched a program of land redistribution as well as nationalising uncultivated land owned by the United Fruit Company, the huge American banana grower. According to Stephen Rabe, "Guatemala's new social welfare programs were more modest than those advocated by liberal Democrats in the United States and Labourites in Great Britain". Indeed, the Arbenz regime stated that the whole point of their land reform programme was designed to undermine the appeal of Communism. Nevertheless, stating that he "couldn't help a government which was openly playing ball with Communists", Eisenhower fully shared Dulles' "deep conviction" that although it was impossible to find evidence tying Arbenz to Moscow, "such a tie must exist". He therefore backed a CIA coup which installed Castillo Armas as a military dictator; Armas proceeded to end land reform and protect American business interests by abandoning Arbenz's nationalisation programme. Stephen Schlesinger therefore regards the Guatemalan coup as "one of the most sordid and inane foreign 'security' operations in American history".

In Cuba and the Dominican Republic, Eisenhower's Cold War policies were more flexible but less successful from his narrow perspective. Eisenhower was shaken by the hostile reception given to his vice-president, Richard Nixon, when he went on a tour of Latin American capitals in 1958: he was stoned and spat on by students in Lima, Peru, then angry mobs attacked his motorcade in Caracas, Venezuela, smashing the windows of his car and nearly overturning it. Eisenhower was finally persuaded by the US State Department that "Anti-communism, as practised by absolute dictators...undermines faith in true democracy". A congressional committee investigating the Nixon trip agreed that the United States should stop creating the impression in Latin America that it was "indifferent to the sufferings of oppressed people". On this basis, Eisenhower started to support trade agreements and generous loans across Latin America. More specifically, he withdrew economic and military aid from Batista in Cuba and Rafael Trujillo of the Dominican Republic.

The result of this new approach was that the dictators of both countries were fatally weakened and ultimately overthrown. After Fidel Castro seized power in Cuba in 1959, Eisenhower initially regarded him as a pragmatic nationalist with whom he could do business, but when the Cuban leader flirted with the Soviet Union, Eisenhower authorised the CIA to "do something about Castro". The ultimate result was the doomed Bay of Pigs invasion in April 1961. Planned during the Eisenhower administration, the operation was carried out under the authority of new President John F. Kennedy, who had taken office just weeks earlier. A force of about 1,400 anti-communist Cuban exiles, supported by the CIA, tried to invade Cuba's south coast, where they erroneously believed the local population would rise up to help them topple Castro's regime. Instead the disastrous attack ended in catastrophic defeat for the CIA-backed forces, badly embarrassing the United States while leaving Castro even more popular and pushing him more firmly into the Soviet camp. Meanwhile, the CIA was implicated in the assassination of Rafael Trujillo, the dictator of the Dominican Republic, in 1961. He had refused to liberalise his regime as the

US demanded ("you can come in here with the Navy or even the atomic bomb, but I'll never go out of here unless I go on a stretcher").

In conclusion, rather than encourage the United States to build stronger and more positive relationships with Latin America, the Cold War tragically persuaded Truman and Eisenhower to adopt a dictatorial and patronising attitude towards their neighbours. As late as 1960, Eisenhower said that the United States would hold "strictly to a policy of non-intervention and mutual respect" but in reality the results of intolerance for any government that leaned toward Communism (whether strongly, like Castro's, or barely at all, like Arbenz's) meant the United States fact did not respect the right of Latin American people to choose their own governments. Human rights and democracy were irrelevant; American Presidents were willing to tolerate and actively support brutal and oppressive dictatorships as long as they declared themselves to be anti-communist.

Cover to the propaganda comic book "Is This Tomorrow"' (1947)

15. HOW DID THE EARLY YEARS OF THE COLD WAR AFFECT THE POLITICAL AND SOCIAL LIFE OF THE UNITED STATES?

The early years of the Cold War had a profound impact upon the political and social life of the United States. Although often described as the era of McCarthyism after its most famous figurehead, Joe McCarthy, the controversial senator for Wisconsin was merely the personification of a deep-seated paranoia which escalated into a full-blown hysteria during the "Second Red Scare". This essay will argue that the most immediate and important social result of the Cold War upon American society was a pervasive climate of fear. This paranoia regarding communism was directly responsible for the political persecution not just of socialists but of any progressives seen as being 'fellow travellers'. Conversely, conservative social campaigners were strengthened due to their anti-communist credentials, as were government security and intelligence agencies such as the CIA and the FBI. The overall result was that in its determination to combat communism, successive US governments eroded the very freedoms which it sought to defend.

The most immediate impact of the Cold War and the growing sense of anti-communism was a climate of fear. The widespread terror that a nuclear conflict between the superpowers would result in the end of civilisation was known as MAD (Mutually Assured Destruction). The Federal Civil Defense Administration was set up in 1950 to prepare the American public for nuclear attacks. Two of the organization's more visible contributions were public fallout shelters and the Emergency Broadcast System, which provided the means by which the President would communicate directly with the public in the event of war. The climate of fear was exacerbated further by public safety films like *Duck and Cover* featuring "Bert the Turtle" and apocalyptic propaganda comic books such as *Is This Tomorrow* (1947).

Another impact of the Red Scare was the abandonment of the left-leaning "New Deal" policies of President Roosevelt. One focus of popular McCarthyism concerned the provision of public health services, particularly vaccination and mental health care, deemed by some to be communist plots to poison or brainwash the American people (the absurdity of which was later satirised by Stanley Kubrick in his film *Dr. Strangelove,* in which the psychotic General Jack D. Ripper becomes convinced that the Soviets are trying to subvert our "precious bodily fluids" through the water fluoridation programme). Ellen Schecker's opinion is that "McCarthyism may have aborted much-needed reforms…The left liberal political coalition that might have supported health reforms and similar projects was torn apart by the anti-Communist crusade".

The persecution of the political left extended to the suspicion of all 'progressives' in society, who were attacked as being 'fellow travellers' of communists, whilst 'conservative' causes found themselves predictably strengthened. The feminist, civil rights and gay rights movements all suffered to varying degrees. In 1951, Elizabeth Gurley Flynn, a pioneer of the American feminist movement, was arrested under the provisions of the Smith Act, which targeted those who called for the overthrow of the US government, and thrown in jail for two years. Flynn was elected as the national chair of the Communist Party in 1961 and visited the Soviet Union several times, where she died in 1964. Paul Robeson, the black musician and civil rights campaigner, was almost lynched upon returning to the USA after a tour of the Soviet Union. A 1950 Senate investigation resulted in the report, *Employment of Homosexuals and Other Perverts in Government*, and in 1953 President Eisenhower issued Executive Order 10450, which meant that homosexuals could be dismissed from federal employment with the reasoning being that they would be particularly susceptible to blackmail in an era of systemic homophobia.

Conversely, 'conservative' causes in society gained a great deal of traction by providing a perceived bulwark against the threat of communism. Two future Republican Presidents made a name for themselves during this period on the back of the Red Scare: Ronald Reagan, who appeared as a 'friendly witness' at the House Unamerican Activities Committee (HUAC) inquiries, and Richard Nixon, who led the case against government official Alger Hiss. The conviction of Hiss damaged those members of the Democratic Party who spoke out in his defence, including, future presidential candidate Adlai Stevenson and Secretary of State Dean Acheson. The conservative religious movement called the Knights of Columbus, fighting against 'godless' communism, even succeeded in persuading Congress to add "under God" to the pledge of allegiance in 1954. Such was the burden of being seen to be 'soft on communism' after his failure in the Korean War that Truman didn't even bother standing for re-election in 1952, preferring instead to step aside as

Eisenhower conducted a political flirtation with McCarthy in his successful campaign for the presidency.

The end result of this growing fear of 'Reds under the Beds' was an erosion of civil liberties as government agencies claimed that this was necessary to protect the people from the threat within. The McCarran Internal Security Act (1950) stipulated that in an emergency, citizens could be imprisoned merely on the suspicion that they might engage in criminal activities. The Immigration and Nationality Act (1952) allowed the government to deport immigrants engaged in subversive activities.

More important still was the development of the CIA and the FBI as anti-communist agencies. The CIA, which focused on combating international threats, is accountable only to the president - there is no democratic or congressional oversight. Its charter allows the CIA to "perform such other functions and duties… as the National Security Council may from time to time direct". This loophole opens the door to covert action and dirty tricks such as the infamous Operation MKUltra. This programme involved mind control experiments including the use of LSD on unwitting participants including drug-addicted prisoners, sex workers and terminally ill patients – "people who could not fight back" in the words of Sidney Gottlieb, the chemist who introduced the hallucinogenic drug LSD to the CIA.

The FBI, which focuses on domestic security and intelligence, operated a secret "Responsibilities Program" that distributed anonymous documents with evidence from FBI files of Communist affiliations on the part of teachers, lawyers, and others. Many people accused in these "blind memoranda" were fired without any further process: 9,500 civil servants were dismissed, 15,000 resigned, and 600 teachers lost their jobs. Even the high-profile scientist Julius Oppenheimer, who had helped develop the atomic bomb in the Manhattan Project, had his security clearance revoked. FBI director Edgar insisted upon keeping the identity of his informers secret; most subjects of loyalty-security reviews were not allowed to cross-examine or know the identities of those who accused them. In many cases they were not even told what they were accused of. The FBI engaged in a number of illegal practices in its pursuit of information on Communists, including burglaries, opening mail and illegal wiretaps. The members of the left-wing National Lawyers Guild were among the few attorneys who were willing to defend clients in communist-related cases, and this made them a particular target of Hoover's. The office of this organization was burgled by the FBI at least fourteen times between 1947 and 1951.

The most pervasive impact of the Cold War upon America was perhaps cultural: the muzzling of a free press and the suppression of a creative film industry. The CIA, in Operation Mockingbird, bribed editors in newspapers around the world to publish pro-American and anti-Communist stories in their publications. More openly, HUAC hounded the "Hollywood Ten" – film executives with suspected communist sympathies – out of the business, with the "Hollywood Blacklist" preventing their employment. As Larry Ceplair and Steven Englund have argued, the investigation of the film industry during the Cold War era was carefully chosen, for "Hollywood was only the tip of an iceberg, but it was a flashing neon tip that captivated the nation's attention". Charlie Chaplin, whose classic film *Modern Times* had shone a critical light upon the dehumanising effects of unregulated capitalism, had his residency permit revoked and had to resettle in Switzerland ("These days", he told one reporter, "if you step off the curb with your left foot, they accuse you of being a Communist"). Arthur Miller was so appalled by the 'witch hunt' in Hollywood that he wrote an allegorical play, *The Crucible,* which was ostensibly a story about the Salem witch trials; it is a thinly disguised critique about how McCarthyism was damaging American society. Many of the resulting films churned out by Hollywood in the years that followed were anti-communist in nature, including *The Manchurian Candidate,* for example, and *Animal Farm,* which was funded by the CIA.

In conclusion, Truman was justified in stating that "McCarthyism…is the corruption of truth…it is the spreading of fear and the destruction of faith in every level of society". A climate of fear diminished progressives and buttressed conservatives; it led to a steady erosion of civil liberties by what Eisenhower would come to describe as a the "military-industrial complex" and threw the cultural life of the USA into a period of stagnation. The final impact of the Cold War upon America was supremely ironic: in an attempt to preserve and defend American values of democracy, the government increasingly eroded all those things in a misguided fear of communist infiltration. The most recent research suggests that McCarthy was not completely incorrect in his accusations – Hiss and Oppenheimer, for example, may perhaps have been guilty of espionage as charged – but the hysteria which he created was out of all proportion to the threat actually posed, and had an immensely negative social and political impact upon the USA for many years to come.

Fulgencio Batista, dictator of Cuba, pictured
during a visit to Washington, D.C., 1951

16. TO WHAT EXTENT WAS CASTRO'S MASTERY OF GUERRILLA WARFARE THE MAIN REASON HE WAS ABLE TO TAKE CONTROL OF CUBA?

Guerrilla warfare can be defined as a form of irregular combat in which a small group of combatants use unconventional military tactics including ambushes, traps, sabotage, and mobility to fight a larger and less-mobile enemy. In the case of Cuba, Che Guevara worked with Fidel Castro to pursue a campaign of "constant mobility, constant vigilance and constant distrust" to defeat the despotic Batista regime in 1959. However, he also recognized that a popular army could only be built up by matching military genius with political acumen. Despite this, Castro's rise cannot be fully explained through reference to the methods he adopted; the conditions within Cuba which he was able to exploit fuelled his revolutionary zeal and propelled him to power.

To some degree it is true that Castro's successful rise to power can be attributed to his mastery of the art of guerilla warfare, although perhaps more credit for this can be given to Che Guevara than to Fidel Castro himself. After all, Castro had originally aimed to gain power through democratic elections.

When this path was closed due to the Batista coup and the subsequent cancellation of the June 1952 elections, he formally protested with a petition known as the *Zarpazo*. When this had no effect he attempted a coup of his own at the Moncada Barracks in 1953, and it was only following his release from prison in 1955 (as a result of Batista's misjudged political amnesty) and his subsequent acquaintance with Che Guevara in Mexico that he was persuaded that guerrilla warfare was the way forward. In 1956 he secretly sailed back to Cuba from Mexico with 80 or so followers in the yacht *Granma*. They were immediately assaulted by Batista's forces and only around 20 of the rebels managed to escape to the relative safety of Sierra Maestra mountains, including Castro himself, his brother Raul, Che Guevara and Camilo Cienfuegos. They were subsequently joined by many others including Vilma Espin and Celia Sanchez. Adopting Che's guerilla mantra of "constant mobility, constant vigilance and constant distrust", they mercilessly executed defectors, but generously welcomed those who joined them - especially former soldiers of Batista who provided much-needed weaponry. As Che put it, guerrillas must extend "the greatest clemency possible toward the enemy soldiers who go into battle performing…their military duty". Consequently, in the Battles of La Plata and Mercedes in 1958, the rebels defeated Batista's larger and better equipped forces and seized control of Havana when Batista fled into exile in January 1959.

As well as military strategies, another essential, and possibly greater aspect of the rebels was the effective use of propaganda to undermine the morale of opponents and win fresh converts within Cuba to the cause. In this respect too, Castro developed considerable mastery. He turned the defeat of the Moncada barracks attack into a victory by delivering his defiant "History Will Absolve Me" speech at his trial and calling his rebel faction the "26th July Movement" after the date of his failed coup; "M-

26-7" then became a prominent slogan of graffiti around Havana. Castro also provided a clear programme of action; his *Five Revolutionary Principles,* developed further in the *Manifesto of the Sierra Maestra,* provided a bedrock of appeal based on specific promises to all groups in society which helped him to secure overall leadership of the rebel movement in the Pact of Caracas (1958). Che established a newspaper (*El Cubano Libre*) and a radio network (*Radio Rebelde*) which broadcast anti-Batista propaganda across Cuba from the "bearded ones" (*Barbudos*) in the Sierra Maestra; Che later claimed this was inspired by CIA operations he observed being used against Jacob Arbenz in Guatemala.

Castro used propaganda to appeal to an international audience, allowing himself to be interviewed by the admiring Herbert Matthews for the New York Times, who stressed that Castro was not a communist, unlike Che (author of *Man and Socialism*). On the contrary, Castro was at pains to persuade his American audience that he "has strong ideas of liberty, democracy, social justice, the need to restore the constitution, to hold elections". In the interview, Castro said, "We are fighting for a democratic Cuba and an end to the dictatorship". These views influenced Roy Rubottom of the US State Department, who wrote a report concluding that "The Cuban Government accuses Castro of being a communist, but has not produced evidence to substantiate the charge". Instead, Castro was presented as a romanticised freedom fighter inspired by the iconic nineteenth-century Cuban nationalist Jose Marti and his twentieth-century equivalent Eduardo Chibás.

Castro made sure that his words were matched by deeds which justified his guerrilla forces describing themselves in the words of Che as a "revolutionary vanguard of the people". The rebels realised the importance of demonstrating "great respect for all the customs and traditions of the people of the zone, in order to demonstrate effectively, through deeds, the moral superiority of the guerrilla fighter over the oppressing soldier" (Che). Castro worked closely with the *Guajiros,* the poorest Cuban peasants to build a base of popular support. His guerrillas always paid for whatever food they took, often at twice the market value. When the guerrillas raided a cattle ranch, they shared their bounty equally with local peasants. Rebel camps held adult literacy classes and organised free medical clinics. This won the support and gratitude of the *Guajiros* to support the rebels; the peasants kept the guerrillas informed of the army's every move.

Nevertheless, despite Castro's clear appreciation that a successful guerrilla campaign consists of military acumen and effective propaganda reflected in genuine social action, his mastery of these tactics does not provide a full explanation of his rise to power. As Che himself later reflected, "Fidel Castro, like any other human being, is the product of history". In this sense, the manifold mistakes, weaknesses and miscalculations of Batista clearly have to be taken into account. Politically, Batista seized power in a military coup shortly before national elections, fearing that the *Ortodoxos* party of which Castro was then a member would win by a landslide. He then cancelled those elections, ignored Castro's formal *Zarpazo* protest, and used his secret police, the BRAC, to treat political prisoners with such brutality that even the CIA expressed its concerns. US Senator John F. Kennedy, later US President, pointed out during the Presidential campaign of 1960 that "Fulgencio Batista murdered 20,000 Cubans in seven years - a greater proportion of the Cuban population than the proportion of Americans who died in both World Wars, and he turned Democratic Cuba into a complete police state - destroying every individual liberty".

Batista's regime was as corrupt as it was violent. He gave favourable trade deals in casinos and hotels to Mafia figures including Meyer Lansky and "Lucky" Luciano. By 1958, US corporations dominated Cuba's economy: The United Fruit Company owned 40% of Cuban sugar exports, US companies controlled 90% of mines, 80% of public utilities, 50% of railways, 25% of bank holdings (about $1 billion), and the Mafia dominated hotels and casinos. Meanwhile, 50% of the population was illiterate and unemployment was 17%. It was clear that the country was being exploited by foreign companies, primarily based in the US, and that Batista worked to continue that system and protect it.

Castro's success in attracting supporters to his guerrilla campaign was, then, due as much to Batista's unpopularity as to his own guerrilla strategies. However, Batista's failings were exacerbated by the thoroughly ambivalent policy of the United States. At first, the Eisenhower administration provided Batista with millions of dollars' worth of military aid and assistance which had allowed him to rule with an iron fist and resist demands for liberalisation. Senator John F. Kennedy, when running for President in 1960, criticised these "short-sighted policies" which "lacked the imagination and compassion to understand the needs of the Cuban people" and instead supported "one of the most bloody and repressive dictatorships in the long history of Latin American repression". Even more critically, however, Eisenhower eventually came to the conclusion that Batista needed to liberalise his regime to ensure its stability, and put pressure on him to do so by withdrawing military aid. However, this simply left the Cuban dictator exposed and vulnerable; a General Strike began in April 1958, which was accompanied by armed attacks from Castro's supporters. Despite sourcing fresh weapons from the United Kingdom, Batista was unable to commit sufficient troops against

Castro in the final critical battles which were conducted under Operation Verano.

In essence, it is clear that Castro's mastery of guerilla warfare clearly provides a central reason why he was able to successfully rise to power. Nevertheless, the fertile ground in which he operated had been created by the dictatorship of Batista, which – thanks in large part to the inconsistent policies of the US presidency – moved from being corrupt, to brutal and then unstable. In this sense it is interesting to consider whether Eisenhower – rather than Castro or Batista – was the individual most responsible for the Cuban Revolution of 1959. Nevertheless, Celia Sanchez was perhaps overly modest when she said that "We rebels get far too much credit for winning the revolution. Our enemies deserve most of the credit, for being greedy cowards and idiots".

A group of demonstrators from *Women Strike for Peace* holding placards relating to the Cuban missile crisis (1962)

17. IS IT FAIR TO SAY THAT AFTER INITIAL FAILURES, KENNEDY'S HANDLING OF FOREIGN POLICY GREW INCREASINGLY SUCCESSFUL AS TIME WENT ON?

Shortly before his death, Kennedy's public approval rating stood at 59%. Directly after his death, another poll ranked him as one of the top three presidents in history. This highlights the fact that in assessing Kennedy's achievements, historians must avoid emotional bias stemming from the fact that he was killed by an assassin's bullet at the peak of his career and with so much potential left unfulfilled. The fact of the matter is that Kennedy had serious initial foreign policy failures in the Bay of Pigs, Vienna and Berlin. Moreover, his success in handling the Cuban Missile Crisis in the middle of his tenure is generally overstated. The end of his presidency was characterised not by success but by the greatest failure of them all: Vietnam.

It is undebatable that with regard to Cuba, Kennedy's initial policy can be described as failure. Kennedy had used Cuba repeatedly in his election campaign, accusing his Republican opponents of being soft on communism, insisting that Cuba was America's "most glaring failure" and one that endangered the "whole Western Hemisphere". Kennedy's ultimate goal, inherited from the Eisenhower administration, was to thoroughly undermine, or even assassinate, Cuban revolutionary leader Fidel Castro. This led to Kennedy's first humiliation; the failed Bay of Pigs invasion of Cuba in April 1961 by anti-Castro Cuban exiles. It was underprepared and underfunded, but as it started to unravel, Kennedy chose to withdraw all support for it rather than get in any deeper, with the result that the 1400 invaders were left to the mercy of the Cuban authorities. Within two days over 100 exiles had been killed and nearly 1,200 had surrendered. Nevertheless, Kennedy continued with what Robert McNamara, his Secretary of Defense, later described as his "hysterical" obsession with Castro, authorising another CIA shambles – Operation Mongoose – which formulated an infamously long list of desperate proposals to assassinate or discredit the Cuban leader: exploding cigars, chemicals to make Castro's beard fall out, and spiking him with hallucinogenic drugs before he delivered a major speech.

The botched invasion left Kennedy in a severely compromised position when he attended the Vienna Summit to discuss the future of West Germany and West Berlin in 1961. The American President was given a hostile reception by the Soviet leader Nikita Khrushchev who dominated the discussions from the outset. These talks centred around the issue of East Germany being declared a sovereign state: a prospect which Kennedy viewed with undisguised alarm since this would place West Berlin – deep in the heart of East Germany - under the direct jurisdiction of the new communist government. The fear was that this regime would unilaterally demand the withdrawal of American, French and British troops from West Berlin, thereby renouncing the four-power agreement reached at Yalta and Potsdam regarding the city's partition into zones of occupation.

Kennedy confided to the journalist Sonny Reston that Khrushchev clearly felt that "anyone who was so young and inexperienced as to get into that mess [the Bay of Pigs] could be taken. And anyone who got into it and didn't see it through had no guts. So he just beat the hell out of me".

A case can also be made, however, that Kennedy's initial failures were increasingly offset by foreign policy successes as time wore on. After all, at Vienna he did not back down in the face of Khrushchev's bluster and threats; the Soviets ultimately backed down on their demands regarding Berlin and instead built the Berlin Wall which, although a human rights abuse on the grand scale, was preferable to war. More assured still was Kennedy's handling of the Cuban Missile Crisis. Upon discovering that the Soviets were installing nuclear bases in Cuba, Kennedy gathered his best advisors, debated the options on how to respond, and then masterfully imposed a "quarantine" - the word "blockade" was deliberately avoided as being too provocative. He explained calmly but forcefully in a TV address where he made it plain that this blatant example of Soviet aggression would not stand. Khrushchev, taken aback by Kennedy's resolve, backtracked humiliatingly, even agreeing that the concessions he gave in return for the removal of the missiles (the US agreeing to remove missiles from Turkey) was kept secret so that Kennedy's reputation would be further enhanced. From this point on, the public perception of Kennedy's foreign policy was of an administration on the top of its game; the crowning moment being the President's visit to Berlin at the end of his presidency where he gave his defiant "Ich bin ein Berliner" speech against the backdrop of the recently constructed Berlin Wall, clearly directed against the Soviet Union.

However, this thesis of an initially unsteady President

rapidly hitting his stride and mastering the art of foreign policy is simplistic. Although Kennedy handled the Cuban Missile Crisis with some assurance, it is also true that the only reason the missile bases were built in Cuba in the first place was firstly because Kennedy had temporarily halted U2 spy plane flights over Cuba after suffering an attack of nerves following the Bay of Pigs. Secondly, because Castro was convinced after this fiasco that another US invasion would take place unless Cuba had a nuclear deterrent. Thirdly, because Khrushchev was convinced after Vienna that Kennedy was weak and would not resist such a development. On this basis the best that can be said of Kennedy with regard to the Cuban Missile Crisis was that he (with Khrushchev's help) successfully cleared up a gigantic mess he was largely responsible for creating.

A similarly mixed picture is presented by Kennedy's "Alliance for Progress", which aimed to establish economic cooperation between the United States and South America. This policy was launched in August 1961 at an inter-American conference at Punta del Este, Uruguay, in the presence of major figures including revolutionary leader Ernesto 'Che' Guevara. The United States pledged to spend $10 billion in the region, over ten years, to build transportation facilities and to provide technology and industrial material. In return, Latin American governments were to institute programmes of social and political reform, including land reform. Kennedy promised that the 1960s would become the "decade of democratic progress" for the region and temporarily broke off relations with several dictatorships in Argentina, the Dominican Republic, Ecuador, Guatemala, Honduras and Peru. The Alliance also helped expand education to disadvantaged communities; nine countries (including Mexico and Brazil, Latin America's largest economies) saw their GDP grow by 2.6% (0.1 percentage point higher than the 2.5% aimed for by the Alliance) during the decade.

Nevertheless, the successes of the Alliance for Progress were outweighed by its failures. First of all, the money made available was limited. The president compared the Alliance to the Marshall Plan but, at the same time, he knew that Congress would never appropriate anything remotely comparable to the funds that were required to rebuild Western Europe after World War II. Secondly, the money that was made available was misspent. Despite costing more than a billion dollars in its first year, not a single Latin American nation committed itself to a comprehensive development program. It is estimated that only 2% of economic growth in 1960s Latin America directly benefited the poor; instead, funds were channelled into military hardware to strengthen repressive regimes. Stephen Rabe notes ironically that although the late 1950s appeared to represent the "twilight of the tyrants", as ten "military dictators fell from power", the 1960s saw sixteen "extra-constitutional changes of government" which led to military rule - the "apogee of military power in Latin America", in the judgement of Michael Gambone. The overall political result was that the Alliance for Progress failed to convince Latin Americans that the USA had magically become more interested in social justice than in propping up loyal but repressive anti-communist dictatorships.

An even stronger argument against Kennedy becoming increasingly successful in foreign affairs comes from an examination of his policy in Vietnam. As in other areas, Kennedy was not responsible for the developing crisis, but certainly exacerbated it and, unlike in Cuba, didn't even resolve it satisfactorily. The Diem regime in South Vietnam had been propped up by the Eisenhower administration with economic aid and military advisors. Kennedy continued the policy despite serious misgivings about the way in which Diem was increasingly acting in a despotic manner against his own people - the most notable group being the Buddhists (Diem was a Catholic), whose highly publicised acts of self-immolation were dismissed by Diem as a "barbecue". To be fair, Kennedy did place pressure on Diem - in an televised interview with Walter Cronkite, he said Diem's policies were "unwise" and that their struggle against the North Vietnamese communists was "their war; they are the ones who have to win it or lose it". However, behind the rhetoric, Kennedy was quietly increasing the number of military 'advisors' (from 900 at the start of his presidency to 16,000 by the end of it) who began herding peasants into "strategic hamlets" which were glorified detention camps seeking to counteract communist infiltration. Worst of all was the fact that through an utter breakdown in communication, Kennedy gave the impression of authorising the badly phrased Hillsman Telegram to Diem's enemies in Vietnam, which seemed to suggest US support for a military coup. When this duly took place and Diem was brutally murdered, Kennedy conducted a political post-mortem where he concluded that "my government is coming apart" and admitted in his phone tapes that "we must bear a great deal of responsibility" for the situation.

Kennedy's foreign policy did not move in a straight line from initial failure to ultimate success. Rather, it can be better described as an arc – moving from initial failure (Bay of Pigs, Vienna and Berlin), through to qualified success (Cuban Missile Crisis, Alliance for Progress) and then ending in ignominious short-term failure in Vietnam with profound long-term consequences for the Johnson administration. Such a view does not fit neatly with the hagiographical perspective of Kennedy historians such as Schlesinger and Sorensen, but highlights that objectivity requires the passage of time. At the end of his life, Robert McNamara was interviewed in the superb documentary

The Fog of War and was at pains to stress the role of accident and human error in Kennedy's foreign affairs; moreover we must beware of treating Kennedy with too much respect due to the tragic manner in which his presidency was cut short. Kennedy's foreign policy started badly, thereby generating the Cuban Missile Crisis, and ended by miring the USA in the most disastrous military engagement in its history. These facts are bleak and inescapable.

Fidel Castro arriving at MATS Terminal, Washington D.C. (1959)

18. BY WHAT METHODS, AND WITH WHAT SUCCESS, DID FIDEL CASTRO TRY TO ELIMINATE DOMESTIC OPPOSITION?

Castro's methods of dealing with domestic opposition can be summarised as a classic 'carrot and stick' approach: undercut the appeal of opponents with forward-looking policies with broad appeal and propaganda, whilst taking a firm line with any critics – perceived or real – to crush dissident forces. His ability to stay in power for more than 40 years demonstrates clear success to some degree, but more pertinent is to question whether oppression or genuine popularity was at the root of this achievement. This essay will argue that Castro's success was based more on genuine popularity than on brutality, but that domestic opposition was never entirely crushed and so the regime he built is increasingly frail in the 21st century.

One method which Castro adopted was to periodically allow opponents to emigrate from Cuba. 250,000 people left the country in the first three years of the Revolution. In 1980, after Cubans pressed into the Peruvian embassy begging for asylum, Castro petulantly dismissed them as "scum" and said that anyone who wanted to leave was free to do so. This led to the Mariel Boatlift, where over a million Cubans voted with their feet and emigrated to the USA. In 1994 too, the government tacitly allowed Cubans to attempt to flee to the US on rafts. These *Balseros* ("rafters") were picked up at sea and interned at the US naval base at Guantanamo Bay. The Clinton Administration, trying to avoid another Mariel, began to limit immigration to the US with those picked up at sea were usually returned to Cuba. As far as Castro was concerned, the propaganda cost of these waves of emigration was offset by the fact that they removed damaging individuals and groups from his island; the Cuban exile community in Florida remains one of the regime's most vocal critics.

In some respects, though, it could be argued that this relaxed attitude towards domestic opposition was rather short-sighted, especially since Castro permanently feared overthrow in the form of a US-sponsored land invasion. This actually transpired in the Bay of Pigs fiasco (authorised by Eisenhower and activated by Kennedy) which failed due to the ineptitude of the invaders as much as any actions by Castro himself. Nevertheless, the fear of invasion continued to haunt Castro, and lay behind his decision to invite the USSR to place nuclear missiles on Cuba, thereby precipitating the Missile Crisis. Although in one sense this strategy for finally neutering the threat of overthrow by Cuban exiles was a failure. After all, the USSR ultimately pulled its missiles out of Cuba, in a deeper sense it consolidated his position by successfully presenting Castro as the defender of Cuban independence in defiance of the United States; Kennedy gave firm assurances to the USSR that there would be no further US attempts to invade Cuba as part of the negotiations which brought the Missile Crisis to an end.

Castro also used more direct political and military methods to control domestic opposition, although these were brutal and damaged his long-term reputation. The regime started bloodily with the show trials and public executions of 500 Batista supporters ("At the smallest of doubt we must execute" – Che). Within his own movement too Castro acted swiftly; he quickly forced the resignations of the President (Urrutia), the head of the Air Force (Lanz) and one of his leading Generals (Matos) from the cabinet for complaining about growing communist influence. Fidel became Prime Minister and his brother Raul took control of the armed forces in his place. In 1965, the regime established prison work camps known as Military Units to Aid Production (UMAP), into which it deposited homosexuals, Jehovah's Witnesses, and other "undesirable" elements which were feared to be instinctively hostile to the regime and its values. In the same year, the Integrated Revolutionary Organisation (ORI) was transformed into the Communist Party of Cuba (PCC), which became the only party permitted. Despite – or perhaps because – of these measures, Castro 'discovered' and imprisoned a "micro-faction" of 37 members led by Anibal Escalante within the PCC opposed to his policies in 1967.

This strong-arm policy continued throughout Castro's rule; in 1980, Cuban human rights activist Ricardo Bofill was sentenced to fourteen years in prison for disseminating "enemy propaganda" and in 1989 Castro ordered General Ochoa shot for 'corruption'. The collapse of the Soviet Union in 1990 made Castro even more defensive. While Castro and hard-liners recognized the need for economic liberalisation, they also saw the likely erosion of political policy and control that accompanies the restructuring of the economy along free-market rules. In February 1999, he introduced the most severe legislation Cuba had ever experienced, condemning dissidents, journalists, and others who deviate from the party line to up to 30 years in prison. Although superficially effective, the brutality of Castro's policies undermined his legitimacy: "With their survival increasingly dependent on a monopoly of raw power…the regime and its leader have lost considerable popular support" (Del Aguila).

In social terms, Castro faced opposition to his authority from artists, writers and educationalists who were more free-thinking than he was willing to allow. At the First Congress of Cuban Writers and Artists (1961), Castro delivered his "words to the intellectuals" where he called upon them to support the Revolution within their work ("within the Revolution, everything; against the Revolution, nothing"). In 1971, the poet Herberto Padilla was tortured into confessing at a show trial to being an enemy of the people. This heralded the "Grey Period" for the arts. The 1976 Constitution stated that "There is freedom of artistic creation as long as it is not contrary to the revolution". A workers' organization, the Confederation of Cuban Workers (CTC) was established to educate and control the workforce. Even the educational game *Monopoly* was banned because it was felt to encourage capitalist competition. Universities de-emphasized the liberal arts or the possibility of active intellectual criticism of major political, social, economic, or cultural problems.

In 1960, Castro set up the Committees for the Defence of the Revolution (CDRs). These are a network of neighbourhood committees across Cuba. CDR officials have the duty to monitor the activities of every person on their respective blocks, and there is an individual file kept on each block resident. Around 80% of the population are members, which is no surprise since scarce resources are allocated according to whether one is a member or not. The other 20% of the adult population are excluded as enemies of the state. Among the most important functions of the CDR are monthly meetings of "political-ideological education circles", during which various materials suggested by the Party leadership are studied and debated. In 1961 Lino Fernandez and 500 members of the underground resistance against the Castro regime were captured and jailed. Three other key opposition leaders were arrested at a meeting in Havana, including Humberto Sorí Marín, the creator of the revolution's Agrarian Reform Law.

Opposition to Castro was therefore effectively quashed before it could gain momentum, but this was perhaps less to do with his strong-arm tactics outlined above than with the fact that he pursued some genuinely positive economic reforms on behalf of the people. Castro's policies initially liberated Cuba from US domination and replaced it with a totalitarian, centrally-planned economy; in 1959, the Urban Reform Act nationalised the largest Cuban factories and the First Agrarian Reform Act nationalised the largest farms. Within months, 200,000 peasants received titles to the land. These farms were later converted into state enterprises on the Soviet model, with the peasants receiving a salary and a small share of profits. The same Act created the Instituto *Nacional de Reforma Agraria* (INRA) and set a limit to landholdings at 1,000 acres. INRA was to organize the land reform, and eventually came to control most rural programs, including health, credit and housing.

Castro also instituted a range of extensive reforms with regard to education, healthcare and women's rights. Free boarding schools were established across the country, which had the additional ideological benefit of breaking down the family unit ("The task of schools…is the ideological formation of revolutionaries" – Castro). In the years that followed, free healthcare was provided for all Cubans in a major programme of reform. Life expectancy at birth in Cuba is now about the same as in the US, despite healthcare spending per capita 5% the size of that of its neighbour. Finally, with regard to women's rights, the Federation of Cuban Women (FMC) was formed under the leadership of Vilma Espín. This trained women to take up new jobs in industry and to lead the literacy campaign in the countryside - "If you do not know, learn; if you know, teach!". By 1986, 80% of all women were members. The Family Code of 1975 equalized the status of husbands and wives, although its success has been limited by deeply ingrained cultural attitudes. Gender parity in the workforce was broadly achieved, although only 14% of party members were women. *Plan Jaba* ('shopping-bag scheme') allowed women to leave a grocery list in the morning and pick up the shopping ready-packed in the evening and established holiday camps and weekend playschemes for children. A Maternity Law was passed in 1974, giving the mother eighteen weeks' paid leave, together with one year's unpaid leave with her job guaranteed if she did not return to work immediately.

Unfortunately for Castro, hopes that these policies would undercut domestic opposition were misplaced. Che Guevara was ideologically stubborn, and his policy of creating the "New Socialist Man" incentivized more by morality than material reward was unrealistic. In Castro's "Revolutionary Offensive" which started in 1968, everyone was paid the same regardless of the quantity or quality or their work. Productivity and efficiency predictably plummeted. Sugar output fell short of planned targets from 1966 to 1970. In 1970 Castro launched the "Ten Million Ton Sugar Crop" initiative, calling upon everybody to get into the fields. Although this produced the largest crop to date, it still fell short of its target by 1.5 million tons, and seriously dislocated the economy in the process. Castro was so damaged by this failure that he offered his resignation in a public meeting, which was rejected with chants of 'Castro!' from the assembled throng. Finally, the collapse of the Soviet Union in 1990 was a devastating blow. Cuba's imports and exports fell by more than 70%. In what he described as the "Special Period", Castro called for Cubans to work harder, sacrifice more, and expect less in the years ahead. Blackouts and public transport restrictions were introduced in response to the disappearance of Soviet oil. In the mid-1990's, Castro reintroduced free market incentives for workers and farmers and increased the number of visas for Cuban-Americans to travel to Cuba to bring in US dollars. Combined with heavy oil subsidies from Venezuela, all of this was economically beneficial but ideologically and politically damaging.

In conclusion, Castro used a combination of intimidation, violence, charm and successful socio-economic policies to buttress his rule and stay in power for more than four decades. On balance, the most crucial of his methods was an enduring ability to pursue reforms clearly designed to improve the life of the ordinary Cuban people, with whom he was usually able to maintain a good rapport – aided in some degree by his use of successful propaganda. Nevertheless, it would be wrong to idealise Castro; he could be brutal, idealistic, and stubborn and self-righteous. For these reasons it can be said that although Castro successfully dealt with domestic opposition, he never succeeded in removing it altogether, with the result that the regime he built is now facing the choice of reforming itself from within, or being overthrown from without.

President Lyndon B. Johnson greeting supporters (1966)

19. HOW SUCCESSFUL WERE PRESIDENT JOHNSON'S "GREAT SOCIETY" REFORMS?

"I will do my best. That is all I can do. I ask for your help – and God's". Lyndon Johnson's modest words to a stunned nation after becoming President following the assassination of John F. Kennedy in 1963 struck a suitably muted note. However, Johnson was a visionary politician who emerged from the shadows of the vice-presidency to unleash the greatest flood of domestic reform legislation since the New Deal policies of his hero, Franklin D. Roosevelt. This achievement is particularly impressive given the various pressures upon him – not least his commitment to the broader Civil Rights struggle and the growing economic and political cost of his government's involvement in the Vietnam War. Nevertheless, Johnson has been criticised for prioritising the quantity of legislation over its quality. Although this criticism has merit, Johnson still deserves great credit not merely for the long-standing success of many of his reforms, but also for the way in which he changed the political dialogue of the United States in terms of the role of the state in society.

In terms of his attempts to improve the cultural life and

horizons of the American people in terms of arts, media and culture, Johnson secured some striking long-term successes. His objective was, in the broadest terms "to advance the quality of our American civilization" by which he meant that an improvement in the general cultural capital of the population would generate life and career opportunities for all citizens, as well as equal access to arts, music and documentary films to allow them to creatively solve problems with an open mind. The National Endowment for the Arts (NEA) supported funding for projects exhibiting artist's excellence. Johnson also established the Public Broadcasting Service, the first public television channel, to bring "knowledge to every corner of the country" (Paula Kerger). PBS still exists today and reaches an estimated 137 million people per month. Johnson felt that all Americans would benefit from cultural enrichment that would provide lifelong learning: "our nation wants more than a 'chicken in every pot'...we want most of all to enrich man's spirit".

A similarly positive picture emerges in education. The key problem which Johnson sought to address was the continued issue of illegal segregation – 10% of the potential workforce (African Americans) were still discouraged from going to school with threats of violence. Beyond this, poor communities simply did not have the economic luxury of being able to value education as a long-term route out of poverty. An estimated 24% of America's children were below the poverty line. The "Head Start" programme – which ultimately benefited 31 million people - gave pre-school education to children from poor communities and also to their parents, allowing both generations to learn together and thereby serving as a community-building project as well as educational purpose. Johnson passed the Elementary and Secondary Education Act of 1965, which granted more than $1 billion for materials and a national Teacher Corps for poverty-stricken areas. Finally, the

Bilingual Education Act of 1968 provided school districts with the federal funds they needed to establish innovative educational programs for students with limited English-speaking ability. Natalia Petrzela observes that the law gave "a shift from the notion that students should be afforded equal educational opportunity to the idea that educational policy should work to equalize academic outcomes, even if such equity demanded providing different learning environments".

Another main pillar of Johnson's Great Society programme was to improve the material well-being of American citizens. In the short term, Johnson bravely brought social deprivation to the centre of the political stage but this was economically unsustainable and ideologically divisive. Johnson declared an "unconditional War on Poverty", stating his objective to be "not only to relieve the symptoms of poverty, but to cure it and, above all, prevent it" – in other words, he billed his program as a "hand-up" and not a "hand-out". In this way, "fighting poverty would save society money in the long run by making unemployed young people and welfare recipients into productive taxpayers" (Robert Dallek). The Office of Economic Opportunity stood at the forefront of the programme, which saw the introduction of the Community Action Program, Job Corps and Volunteers in Service to America (VISTA), and food stamps to help low-income families supplement their diets with healthy foods.

On the negative side, during Johnson's administration - a period when the economy was continually growing - the public assistance rolls in New York City nevertheless tripled from around three hundred thousand to more than a million people. According to Republicans, this was because the incentive to find work evaporated and was replaced instead with a desire to take advantage of Johnson's profligacy. In the long run too, poverty remains a problem: in 2015 an estimated 13.5% of the US population was in poverty. Therefore by Johnson's own criteria the War on Poverty has been a failure, although the core reason for this is debatable: whilst the aim to make poor people self-sufficient was a noble one, his opponents would argue that it could not be achieved merely by throwing money at a problem and creating a "welfare trap". In contrast, his supporters would point to the cuts made to his programmes by successive Republican administrations.

A similarly mixed picture is evident with regard to Johnson's reforms of the health system. When Johnson came to power, it was estimated that 20% of Americans had, due to financial pressures, never been to a doctor or been treated at a hospital. Moreover, half of the elderly had no health insurance due to its prohibitive cost. To combat these problems, Medicare and Medicaid were introduced in 1965 under the Social Security Act. Medicare provided immediate federal funding of essential medical costs for 19 million senior citizens. Medicaid served the same purpose for low-income families. Moreover, the Maternal and Child Health programme provided family planning services along with pre- and ante-natal care with the result being that the infant mortality rate dropped by 12% decline in just four years. In total Johnson passed 49 major pieces of legislation in the social welfare field.

Nevertheless, the quantity of health legislation affected its quality. Laws were rushed through Congress and so loopholes were left in place which undermined their effectiveness. For example, it is quite clear that Johnson woefully underestimated basic costs. Democratic Congressman Wilbur Mills, despite being a great supporter of the programme, commented that its estimated national cost in the first year was $250 million, but in actual fact this much was spent in New York alone. Moreover,

Johnson failed to anticipate that government largesse would enable drug companies and medical equipment suppliers to inflate the price of their products, confident that the government would pick up the bill. Another problem was that doctors were not obliged to treat Social Security patients and so 25% of them refuse to do so in favour of private patients, placing pressure on hospital casualty wards. Finally, eligibility for Medicaid was not linked to the federal poverty level, but instead had such a stricter requirement that 60% of citizens below the official poverty line are still denied assistance.

A comparable pattern of grand legislation marred by an inattention to detail can be seen with reference to environmental legislation. Johnson, working alongside his wife, "Lady Bird", certainly deserves credit for being one of the first mainstream politicians to take an interest in the environment; in 1965, at the inaugural White House Conference on National Beauty, he said that "The air we breathe, our water, our soil and wildlife, are being blighted...The society that receives the rewards of technology, must, as a cooperating whole, take responsibility for [their] control". The Clean Air Act of 1963 created a research and regulatory program in the U.S. Public Health Service. the Wilderness Protection Act of 1964 saved 9.1 million acres of forestland from industrial development, the Motor Vehicle Air Pollution Control Act of 1965 set the first federal vehicle emissions standards, and the National Trails System Act of 1968 created national scenic and recreational trails "to promote the preservation of, public access to, travel within, and enjoyment and appreciation of the open-air, outdoor areas and historic resources of the Nation". However, in some key respects his environmental record can be criticised for its lack of effectiveness. With regard to the Wilderness Protection Act, only 28 out of more than 2,000 endangered species are due to recover: a success rate of 1%. In some respects, this legislation was counterproductive as it encouraged pre-emptive habitat destruction by landowners who fear losing their land because of the presence of an endangered species, a phenomenon known as "shoot, shovel and shut up".

Overall, Johnson's obsession with simply passing as many new laws as quickly as possible and hoping that their loopholes would magically sort themselves out was a naïve miscalculation for such a famously shrewd politician. Johnson himself perhaps recognized the limitations of his achievements after his retirement in 1971, commenting that "I figured when my legislative program passed the Congress that the Great Society had a real chance to grow into a beautiful woman…It's a terrible thing for me to sit by and watch someone else starve my Great Society to death". Nevertheless, he achieved some major successes, especially in cultural terms, and we should remember that this was every bit as important a part of the Great Society as the drive to improve material standards. As Johnson himself put it: "The Great Society … is a place where the city of man serves not only the needs of the body…but the desire for beauty and the hunger for community". In this respect, President Obama was surely right when he recently commented that "These endeavours didn't just make us a better country. They reaffirmed that we are a great country".

Vietnam War protestors march at the Pentagon in Washington, D.C.
October 1967.

20. TO WHAT EXTENT WAS GUERRILLA WARFARE THE MAIN CAUSE OF COMMUNIST VICTORY IN VIETNAM?

The division of Vietnam along the 17th parallel in the aftermath of World War Two set the scene for one of the bloodiest conflicts of the twentieth century. Both Ho Chi Minh in the communist North, and Ngo Dinh Diem in the capitalist South, were determined to unite the entire country under their personal rule. The assassination of Diem in 1963 created a power vacuum which drew the United States ever more deeply into South Vietnam, whilst the North gained the support of Communist China and the USSR. However, this was a conflict which not only pitted the superpowers against each other, but also involved horrific civilian casualties within Vietnam and mass demonstrations against the American government until its troops were finally pulled out of the country in 1975. This essay will argue that guerilla warfare strategies bewildered American presidents, who had surprisingly failed to learn any meaningful lessons from their recent experiences in Korea. The military quagmire was publicised by the American media, which in turn generated a degree of opposition which made the war impossible to win.

During a televised interview in the Sierra Maestra in 1970, Fidel Castro said that the success of the North Vietnamese communists was the result of the same guerrilla strategies which he had used to overthrow the Batista regime in 1959. After all, although under Ho Chi Minh they had a regular army (the ARVN) it was the irregular guerrilla forces of the Vietcong that wreaked havoc on the South Vietnamese forces and their US allies for the duration of the war. Confronted with an enemy that was superior in terms of manpower and military hardware, the Vietcong adopted a bewildering array of strategies to compensate. For example, *Punji* traps consisted of sharpened sticks tipped with excrement and plunged into shallow holes which were covered by grass and sticks; any soldier falling into these would be impaled and infected. An elaborate network of tunnels was created which enabled Vietcong fighters to appear and disappear at will to launch surprise attacks. Finally, the Ho Chi Minh trail allowed supplies to reach the Vietcong forces via Cambodia and Laos, two countries that the US at first did not want to attack to stop the Vietcong for fear of escalating the conflict further and possibly deepening China's involvement.

These guerrilla strategies were not only militarily significant in themselves, but also in the effect that they had upon the morale and conduct of the American campaign. Operation Rolling Thunder, which began in 1965, consisted of a monumental bombing campaign of North Vietnam, combined with the use of such horrific weapons as Agent Orange (a poisonous defoliant) and Napalm (liquid fire). These can be seen as a desperate attempt to fight an invisible guerrilla enemy, as can the "Search and Destroy" missions which consisted of burning entire villages to the ground on the basis that anyone and everyone within them could possibly be Vietcong. All of this did the exact opposite of helping the US win the "hearts and minds" of the Vietnamese people. The most notorious example of the inhumanity of this policy was the Mai Lai Massacre (1968), exposed in a newspaper piece by Seymour Hersh and publicised by a widely reported court martial which highlighted the dehumanising effect that American responses to guerrilla warfare were having upon American soldiers. Moreover, mainstream media turned against the administration after the Tet Offensive of 1968, which saw the Vietcong launching attacks within the South Vietnamese capital of Saigon and even briefly invading the American Embassy. Walter Cronkite, the CBS anchorman known as "the most trusted man in America" returned from Vietnam and broke all impartiality conventions by delivering the following damning verdict: "To say that we are closer to victory today is to believe, in the face of the evidence, the optimists who have been wrong in the past. To suggest we are on the edge of defeat is to yield to unreasonable pessimism. To say that we are mired in stalemate seems the only realistic, yet unsatisfactory, conclusion". Johnson was devastated by the report, despairing that "If I've lost Cronkite, I've lost Middle America".

This loss of media support within the USA highlights that guerrilla warfare strategies had a wider impact beyond Vietnam itself. Crucially, this was the first televised war. Scenes of villages being burned, and of American soldiers thrashing their way inch by inch through jungles laden with booby traps, had a profound effect on the nation's self-perception. For the first time, Americans were confronted with the unpleasant realisation that maybe they weren't always on the side of freedom and democracy, but were slipping into an attitude of imperial arrogance and the mantra that 'might is right'. As a result, social protests on an unprecedented scale destabilised and distracted the American government from fighting an effective military campaign. Hunkering down in the White House, President

Johnson had to listen to crowds of protestors chanting daily "Hey, Hey, LBJ, how many kids have you killed today?". These protests also involved musicians (from Barry McGuire's *Eve of Destruction* to Country Joe McDonald's *Feel like I'm Fixin' to Die*), sportsmen (Muhammad Ali's refusal to honour the draft with the words "No Vietcong ever called me n*gger") and even prominent civil rights figures including Martin Luther King's impassioned *Beyond Vietnam* speech, wherein he stressed how the war was distracting the Johnson administration from its "Great Society" social reform programmes. Students too protested loudly and continuously; this movement reached its crescendo when National Guardsmen shot dead several students at Kent State University in 1970 - an event immortalised by Neil Young in his song *Ohio*, which he recorded directly afterwards. This vocal and outraged minority of Americans drowned out what Nixon later called the "Silent Majority" who passively or actively supported the war and made it increasingly difficult to present a united front.

However, although these social protests can be seen as a result of American confusion, bewilderment and inability to fight a guerrilla warfare in a far-flung continent, they were nevertheless also the product of a weak political leadership which itself demonstrated itself incapable of rising to the situation. Johnson in particular had a misguided way of dealing with social opposition, adopting what he referred to as a policy of "minimum candour" in his handling of the press corps whilst at the same time giving them unfettered access to military engagements in Vietnam itself – a toxic combination creating a "credibility gap" for his administration. More fundamentally, Johnson lacked the political objectivity to understand the motives of the people he was fighting. Looking through the Cold War prism of 'Containment' and 'Domino Theory', he saw the Vietcong as communist puppets of China and the Soviet Union who could easily be beaten into submission by force of arms. In reality, the Vietnamese primarily saw communism as a tool for overthrowing the illegal and corrupt Saigon regime that was being propped up by US imperialism and as a nation that had been resisting Chinese colonisation for more than a thousand years, they were nobody's stooges. This lack of empathy and political and historical insight explains the blunt military response which dragged the USA into a hellish quagmire. Operation Rolling Thunder was an attempt to bomb the Vietcong to the negotiating table, whereas in fact it merely galvanised their determination to resist. President Johnson, relying on the advice of his "wise men" including Robert McNamara and Dean Acheson, lacked the self-confidence in diplomatic terms to chart another course, and then found himself abandoned by them towards the end of his administration. President Nixon pursued the much more creatively flexible approach of using China and the USSR to put pressure on Hanoi through "Triangular Diplomacy". However, it was still another seven years before the war came to an unsatisfactory conclusion, during which time Nixon and Kissinger continued to make the same blunt military mistakes as Johnson – even escalating the bombing into neighbouring Laos and Cambodia in their "Operation Menu" campaigns.

To sum up, guerilla warfare and the political inability of American presidents to find an appropriate response to it was a main cause of communist victory in Vietnam. This in turn undercut domestic support for the war to a degree which made it impossible to maintain. Despite its experiences in Korea, the USA had an imperfect understanding of the demands of guerilla warfare and responded with a level of frustrated brutality which undermined the morale of its own soldiers and civilians at the same time that it steeled the resistance of their communist enemies. The Paris Peace Accords signed in 1973 (followed by the final US troops withdrawn in 1975) were described by Nixon as "Peace with Honour" but in reality they represented a profound failure of US foreign policy objectives. More positively, it also led to a paradigm shift in Cold War strategy: for a generation or more, "Vietnam Syndrome" meant that American presidents became much more circumspect about the efficacy of military intervention to secure regime change, especially in faraway lands inhabited by people who had mastered the arts of guerrilla warfare.

Francisco Franco and his wife, Carmen Polo, May 1968

21. HOW SUCCESSFULLY DID FRANCO ACHIEVE HIS OBJECTIVES AS RULER OF SPAIN, 1939-75?

As inscrutable as he was unscrupulous, General Francisco Franco is one of the most enigmatic of the twentieth century's many dictators. As ruler of Spain from the moment of his victory in the Spanish Civil War of 1939 to his death in 1975, he came to power determined to lead a one-party state which would restore what he saw as traditional Spanish values – including Castilian culture, the Catholic religion, and clearly defined gender roles. However, as time wore on the necessity of opening up Spain to foreign influence in terms of international recognition and economic investment compelled him to moderate his slogans and liberalise his policies. As a result, by the end of his life Spain was diplomatically secure and thriving economically; this opening of the floodgates, however, changed Spanish society and culture to such a degree that the political regime he had established failed to survive beyond his death.

In political terms, Franco's short-term brutality fostered underground separatist extremism. All opposition parties were banned and the National Movement (*Movimiento Nacional*) became the only permitted channel for political discourse in Spain. "The Movement", as it became known, was a collective name for the main political interest groups in Francoist Spain: the Falangist political class, the workers' syndicates, the army, and the Catholic Church. The first decade of Franco's rule in the 1940s following the end of the Civil War in 1939 saw continued oppression and the killing of thousands of political opponents. The Law of Political Responsibilities (1939) gave such wide powers to the *Caudillo* that in the first three months of his rule alone 250,000 people were arrested. In July 1947, a law was passed that made Franco head of state for life, and subsequently his state became less murderous. Nevertheless, political dissidents of all persuasions continued to be violently suppressed.

More positively, in 1969 Franco made arrangements which he hoped would ensure a peaceful transition of power after his death, although without any desire to dilute that power with democratic reforms. He announced that the Bourbon monarchy would be restored, but that the throne would be passed not to the first in line Don Juan (a liberal who had a prickly relationship with the Francoist regime), but to his 31-year-old son Juan Carlos. In 1975, General Franco died and King Juan Carlos acceded to the throne, although his father only renounced his own claim in 1977. To his credit, Juan Carlos immediately began dismantling the Francoist dictatorship and won support in the 1978 referendum for a new Spanish constitution which transformed Spain into a constitutional monarchy.

With regard to cultural affairs, Franco's Spanish nationalism promoted a unitary national identity and quashed Spain's cultural diversity. Franco aimed, in his own words, "to enforce a brand of traditionalist and authoritarian Spanish nationalism that harboured no expression of the distinct 'minority cultures'".

Bullfighting and flamenco were promoted as national traditions while those traditions not considered "Spanish" were suppressed. Catalonia, which had a strong national identity and which had come out strongly against Franco in the Civil War, was subject to particularly harsh measures. The Catalan language, its national dance (the *Sardana*) and Catalan Christian names were forbidden. Castilian Spanish was the only officially recognised language and its use in public life and in schools became compulsory: other languages such as Catalan, Basque and Galician were "confined to private spaces" and disparaged as "dialects". In protest at these policies, 1959 a group of intellectuals created a Basque separatist movement named ETA (*Euskadi Ta Askatasuna* - "Basque Homeland and Liberty"). ETA evolved into a violent terrorist organisation which, in 1973, assassinated Admiral Carrero Blanco - who had recently been appointed Prime Minister by the ailing Franco.

Francoism also adopted a reactionary conservatism with regard to the role of women in society. Feminism was castigated as a form of Marxist depravity and the progressive laws passed by the Second Republic promoting sexual equality were repealed. The organisation placed in charge of preparing women for their role as wives, mothers, Catholics and patriots was the Women's Section of the Falange (*Sección Femenina de Falange*). This was led by Pilar Primo de Rivera (sister of José Antonio, who had established the fascist Falange party during the Second Republic, and daughter of Primo, the dictator who ruled Spain before it). In one 1944 edition of *Semanario*, its official magazine, the Women's Section declared that "The life of every woman, despite what she may pretend, is nothing but a continuous desire to find somebody to whom she can succumb. Voluntary dependency, the offering of every minute, every desire and illusion is the most beautiful thing". Women needed permission to do the most basic of activities, including opening a bank account or going on a trip; many jobs in law and education were closed to them. The Women's Section provided a helpful daily timetable to help housewives organise themselves: an endless round of cleaning, cooking, washing and errands. To those that worried that this continual menial drudgery would undermine their child-bearing fitness, the state-sponsored magazine *Teresa* reassured readers that "A woman who has to attend to household chores regularly has the opportunity to do as much gymnastics as she will never truly do if she worked outside her home…cleaning and polishing the floors is a very effective example".

With regard to religion, Catholicism was upheld as the established church of the Spanish State, and so regained many of the traditional privileges it had lost under the Republic. The Jesuit Order, suppressed during the Spanish Second Republic, returned and once again took over the education of students. Bishops took their place in parliament and new laws corresponded to Catholic doctrine. Civil servants had to be Catholic, and some official jobs even required a "good behaviour" reference from a priest. Civil marriages which had taken place under Republican Spain were declared invalid unless confirmed by the Catholic Church. Divorce was forbidden, as were contraceptives and abortion. Declaring Spain to be "One of the great spiritual reserves of the world", Franco signed a Concordat with the Vatican in 1953 and Pope Pius XII congratulated him for his defence of "the ideals of faith and Christian civilization". Franco was personally a man of impeccably traditional religious convictions; according to Stanley Payne, he "believed devoutly in the efficacy of relics, his personal favourite being the remains of a petrified arm of Saint Teresa of Avila which he had obtained in the Civil War and kept on a bedstand for the remainder of his life".

In the diplomatic realm, Franco's official neutrality in World War Two was not initially enough to prevent Spain's international isolation, although Cold War tensions meant that this was not a prolonged inconvenience. In 1945, the "Big Three" victorious powers – the UK, the USA and the USSR - blocked Spanish entry into the newly constituted United Nations, stating that "The three governments…will not support any request for accession (in the UN) to the present Spanish Government, which [was] established with the support of the Axis powers". The following year the UN formally adopted Resolution 39 to this effect, pointing to Franco's seizure of Algiers in 1940 and deployment of the Blue Legion to fight alongside the Nazis in Soviet Russia as evidence of his perfidy.

Nevertheless, Francoist Spain did not remain a diplomatic pariah for long. As Cold War tensions increased, the United States increasingly saw him (as the British and French had seen Hitler in the 1930s) as a useful potential ally against the spread of communism. As early as 1950, the appointment of a US ambassador to Madrid was announced. In 1955, John Foster Dulles, America's highly influential Secretary of State, paid him a visit. In the same year Spain's application to join the United Nations was accepted – although membership of NATO and the European Economic Community would have to wait until after his death because Western European states remained more circumspect in their regard for Spain than did the United States. By 1956, relations were also thawing with the Soviet Union, which repatriated 4,000 Spanish nationals who had been displaced by the Civil War. As his rule proceeded, Franco appeared less frequently in military uniform, preferring instead sharply cut civilian suits in order to create a visual distance between the soldier of the civil war and the statesman he now claimed to be.

Franco's diplomatic rehabilitation brought economic benefits. Spain had emerged from the civil war catastrophically compromised and initially isolated from international trade. National income had reverted back to 1914 levels and 60% of Spain's rolling stock had been destroyed. Even ten years later real wages were only at half the level they had been at the outbreak of the war and rationing would remain in place until 1952, giving rise to a thriving but illegal black market – the *Estraperlo*. Franco's initial response to this economic chaos was to use political prisoners as slave labour. Former Republicans were organised into "labour battalions" to rebuild Spanish infrastructure - roads, bridges, dams – and even to construct the gigantic mausoleum to Franco in the *Valle de los Caidos* (Valley of the Fallen), which took twenty years to complete. In addition, strikes and non-government trade unions such as the UGT and CNT were banned, the latter being replaced with the Spanish Syndical Organization (*Sindicato Vertical*) to which all workers had to belong. In 1951, the continuing stagnation of the Spanish economy led to an illegal mass strike involving hundreds of thousands of workers in Barcelona, but as Spain emerged from her diplomatic isolation in that decade, the economic landscape began to improve markedly. In 1953 Franco signed the Pact of Madrid with the USA which, in return for considerable financial aid ($ 1.8 billion by 1965), gave the Americans use of Spanish military bases. The influx of dollars was soon felt in the Spanish economy, which experienced a "long boom" which became known as the "Spanish Miracle". The 1960's was a prosperous time for Spain with industry and commerce finding international markets: the car manufacturer, SEAT, brought prosperity back to Barcelona, for example.

The "Spanish Miracle" evinced itself most clearly in a burgeoning tourist market. Franco took a keen personal interest in this area: rather bizarrely, he had marketed tourist trips of civil war battlefields, for example, even before the conflict had ended. Spain was blessed with a vast expanse of virgin coastline that was quickly developed (and much of it eventually ravaged) with hotels and apartment blocks that were cheap by European standards. Benidorm, a sleepy village of fishermen and farmers on the Mediterranean coast in the 1960s, became the archetypal resort for mass tourism. Under the slogan "Spain is Different", the number of foreign visitors jumped from 4.3 million in 1960 to 30 million by 1975. Tourism ensured that Spain "rode a tide of ever-increasing national prosperity" (Stanley Payne) but also played an important role in Spain's democratic development: it brought Spaniards into contact with different peoples and ideas, particularly from European democracies, and broadened their horizons. At a time when many females still dressed in black from head to toe, the appearance of foreign women in miniskirts and bikinis was nothing short of revolutionary.

In the final analysis, Franco's reactionary aims for society and culture were fundamentally incompatible with his progressive desire for international legitimacy and economic growth. Attracting diplomatic recognition and foreign investment necessitated liberalising his regime both economically and politically as well as opening his country up to social and cultural influences which ran counter to 'traditional' Spanish values. By the time of his death, mass tourism and international trade had brought prosperity to Spain, but this economic miracle ironically meant that the Spain he had fought to preserve had largely ceased to exist. Within a few years of his death, Spain had become a constitutional monarchy, although the abortive military coup that was launched in his name in 1981 reflected the deep fault lines upon which his regime was built, and which still haunt Spain and his reputation today.

Albert Howard at a Black Panther meeting, January 1970

22. FOR WHAT REASONS, AND WITH WHAT RESULTS, DID THE US CIVIL RIGHTS MOVEMENT BECOME MORE RADICAL AFTER 1964?

Before 1965 the US Civil Rights movement was based primarily in the South and focused on achieving full integration for Black Americans (in the spirit of William DuBois and championed by Martin Luther King) through the use of nonviolence. After 1965, however, it was increasingly based in the North and focused on achieving a separate black society (in the spirit of Marcus Garvey, championed by Malcolm X) through violent action if necessary. The reasons for this change can be explained by a new outlook provided by Malcolm X and others, who were in turn responding to the fact that the pace of change was too slow, in the wrong direction, and at the expense of black lives.

One way in which the movement changed was away from a philosophy of nonviolence, as promoted by King, towards a belief in the militant of self-defence, as promoted by Malcolm X and practised by the Black Panthers. The first phase of the Civil Rights movement is indelibly associated with Martin Luther

King. He led the Southern Christian Leadership Conference (SCLC) which used nonviolent boycotts, demonstrations and marches (such as those on Washington and Selma) to raise awareness, provoke a racist backlash, and thereby force the federal government into action. The first phase was also dominated by other organisations such as the National Association for the Advancement of Colored People (NAACP), which worked through the courts to mount legal challenges to segregation in education (e.g. the Brown v. Board of Education case) and transport (e.g. the Montgomery Bus Boycott). However, whereas King and other activists from this first phase of the movement favoured nonviolence, the NAACP and SCLC was sidelined in the later 1960s by a newly radicalized Student Nonviolent Coordinating Committee (SNCC), which had organised the "Freedom Rides", and the Committee for Racial Equality (CORE), which had organised the "Freedom Summer" voting registration campaign. By the mid-1960s, this new breed of activists was starting to be drawn to the philosophy of Malcolm X, who suggested that nonviolent resistance was "the philosophy of the fool" and advocated self-defence "by any means necessary", arguing that "it is criminal to teach a man not to defend himself, when he is the constant victim of brutal attacks...I don't call it violence when it's self-defence, I call it intelligence".

The first reason why the civil rights movement shifted towards militant self-defence is that many activists became convinced that nonviolence had run its course. During the Birmingham Campaign of 1963, activists had met with the unremitting brutality of "Bull" Connor; in the Freedom Summer Campaign of 1964 three civil rights workers were lynched. There was specific disillusionment with King in particular, especially following the humiliation of "Turnaround Tuesday" where King called off one of the 1965 Selma Marches to avoid further bloodshed after clashes with the police during "Bloody Sunday". The trigger event which radicalized the movement was the "March Against Fear" (1966) when there was a division between those aligned with King (who used the slogan "Freedom Now") and those aligned with Malcolm X's natural heir Stokely Carmichael (who instead adopted "Black Power") and stated that "a 'non-violent' approach to civil rights is an approach black people cannot afford and a luxury white people do not deserve!".

This new belief in the legitimacy of militant self-defence manifested itself in two clear ways. Firstly, and most destructively, the result was a spate of violence across America engulfing cities such as Watts (1965) and Detroit (1967). In 1968, the assassination of King provoked a fresh wave of violence in Washington, Chicago and Baltimore. Secondly, the Black Panthers emerged under the leadership of such figures as Huey Newton, Fred Hampton and Bobby Seale. The Panthers exploited "open carry" laws to tail police patrols whom they suspected of harassing black communities. This in turn provoked a violent response from the authorities. J. Edgar Hoover, director of the FBI, described the Panthers as the "greatest threat to the internal security of the country". Under Operation COINTELPRO, he set out to crush the Panthers before a "Black Messiah" emerged. Bobby Seale was gagged and tied to a chair during his trial, Huey Newton was thrown in jail and Fred Hampton and Bobby Hutton were gunned down by law enforcement officers.

The second key change in the nature of the Civil Rights movement in the second half of the 1960s was a move away from integration as the ultimate goal in favour of a separation of the races. The early leaders of the movement had campaigned against segregation and, therefore, in favour of integration.

However, Malcolm X in contrast adopted the black nationalism earlier championed by Marcus Garvey, which envisaged black control of the social, economic, and political institutions in black communities. More generally, black nationalism was characterised by a belief that black people should embrace and celebrate their African heritage rather than seek acceptance of the white man by mimicking his values, behaviour and even appearance. It was on this basis that Malcolm X abandoned his "slave name" of Malcolm Little and went on a tour of African states to generate support for the Organisation for the Afro-American Unity, which he hoped would work through the United Nations to shame the US into dealing with its race problem. After Malcolm's assassination in 1965, this philosophy was taken up by the "Black Power" movement, spurred by Stokely Carmichael, who rejected the "thalidomide drug of integration"; like Malcolm, he reached out to his African roots, changing his name to Kwame Ture and marrying the legendary anti-apartheid musician Miriam Makeba. It is particularly important to note that by the end of his life even King was reconsidering the efficacy of integration ("We have fought hard and long for integration…but I have come to believe that we are integrating into a burning house").

The reason why the ultimate goal of activists shifted in this way from integration to separation was firstly because there was a growing belief that racist attitudes and institutions were too deeply entrenched in American society for legislation-based integration to ever work. John Griffin, in *Black Like Me,* had pointed out in the 1950s that integration could lead to a sense of "fragmented individualism" for black people who would never be fully accepted by the white community but would nevertheless alienate themselves from their black culture in their desperate attempts to integrate. The generational divide which had split the movement with regard to the issue of nonviolence also has its equivalent with regard to the integration debate: the charismatic young boxing champion Muhammad Ali, easily the most famous black American in the world by the mid-1960s, had become a fervent proponent of black nationalism ("Integration is wrong"). Ali's belief in black nationalism, and that of many other younger activists, was consolidated by the Vietnam War: when President Johnson used the draft to swell the ranks of soldiers being sent to fight in Vietnam for the cause of democracy and freedom, many blacks baulked at the hypocrisy of being asked to fight a white man's war in Asia for a government which treated them with contempt: as Muhammad Ali most famously put it, "No Vietcong ever called me n*gger". Stripping Ali of his titles merely made him a martyr to the cause, as reflected in the famous *Esquire* cover image of him as St. Sebastian, tied to a stake and covered with arrows.

The results of this shift expressed themselves in sport, women's rights and music. In sport, one of the most spectacular and unexpected demonstrations for Black Power occurred at the 1968 Summer Olympics in Mexico City. At the conclusion of the 200m race, at the medal ceremony, United States gold medallist Tommie Smith and bronze medallist John Carlos wore Olympic Project for Human Rights badges and showed the raised fist – the Black Power salute - as the anthem played. In terms of the Black Panthers, women made up nearly two-thirds of the party's membership and demonstrated the growing realization that women's voices were integral to the continuing campaign for equal rights. Kathleen Cleaver, the most iconic of the female Black Panthers, led a campaign which sought to persuade women to be proud of their natural hair by cultivating an 'Afro', bemoaning the fact that black women "were told that only white people were beautiful - that only straight hair, light eyes, light skin was beautiful." This "Black is Beautiful" movement was echoed in the music of the period, including *Say it Loud: I'm Black and I'm Proud!* (James Brown) and *To be Young, Gifted and Black* (Nina Simone).

The change in methods (towards militant self-defence) and objectives (separation, not integration) overlapped with two further shifts in focus for the civil rights movement. Firstly, in socio-economic terms there was a vigorous movement away from the rural south and towards the urban north. The traditional movement, which originated in the Southern states, had focused on legal challenges to segregation as the way forward for the black population; but by the mid 1960s the problems of urban poverty, ghettoised segregation and lack of education opportunities in the northern states especially were gaining wider attention compared to the traditional issues of discrimination in the south. There was the growing feeling that economic injustice, not state laws in themselves, were the root cause of racism that needed to be tackled but that this would involve revolutionary action. By 1968, even King had sadly reached the conclusion that "Urban riots must now be recognized as durable social phenomena" and that the struggle for integration would ultimately become a struggle for economic rights: "Capitalism does not permit an even flow of economic resources...a small privileged few are rich beyond conscience and almost all others are doomed to be poor at some level…And since we know that the system will not change the rules, we're going to have to change the system".

The main reason for this change in geographical focus is that for all their high-flying rhetoric, President Johnson's Great Society programmes had failed to deliver the level of change which raised expectations had led people to expect. Although the Civil Rights Act of 1964 had ended *de jure* (legal) segregation in the South, it had done nothing to end and *de facto* (actual) segregation, discrimination and violence in either the South or the North. Moreover, although black Americans could vote freely following the Voting Rights Act of 1965, many still faced severe economic hardship and poor educational systems and housing compared with whites, which in turn limited their life chances and job prospects. Therefore, by the end of his life even King was spending an increasing amount of time leading campaigns in urban centres like Chicago, and delivering impassioned speeches such as "Beyond Vietnam" where he openly criticised the government for finding the money to fight Vietcong in Asia at the same time that it claimed there was no money to properly deal with issues of poverty within black communities in America.

The immediate result of this new focus on the structural economic problems of the north instead of the immorality of segregation in the south was the government-appointed Kerner Commission (1967) to investigate the nature of the problem. This federal investigation of the race riots which blighted the second half of the decade concluded that the United States was becoming "two societies, one black, one white – separate but unequal" due to systemic racism in the United States. The second result was to give further impetus to the Black Panthers, who defined themselves as revolutionary Marxists seeking to establish socialism through mass organizing and community-based programs ("We believe our fight is a class struggle and not a race struggle" – Bobby Seale). Their Ten-Point Program focused heavily on social and economic justice; their Free Breakfast Program for the poorest black children fed 10,000 students every single day at its height.

The move towards militant self-defence and black nationalism also reflected and effected changes in the religious complexion of the struggle. The traditional leadership of the movement centred around the churches, which is understandable not only on religious grounds as agreed by Vicki Phipps - "oppression, rejection and segregation leave a human being with no one to turn to, but God". Churches were also important because they were the only places where black communities could legally congregate in large numbers. Therefore, figures such as King, Ralph Abernathy and Fred Shuttlesworth – Baptist preachers who formed the SCLC – had taken a prominent leadership role alongside lawyers of the NAACP and moderate figures such as Roy Wilkins of CORE. However, from Malcolm X onwards a number of civil rights figures moved away not just from the traditional leadership of the SCLC, but from Christianity altogether.

The main reason for this shift away from Christianity within the movement is that the stress on nonviolence and integration was increasingly seen by some radicals as being symptomatic of Christian submissiveness and insufficiently strong to counteract the deep-seated racism at the heart of society. Arguably, the movement's Christian morality and dependence on dramatizing the immorality of segregation through acts of nonviolent civil disobedience were insufficient when confronted with deeper and more systemic inequalities in American society. In the words of Paul Harvey, "To those stuck in poverty, the right to eat a hamburger at a lunch counter was not particularly meaningful".

The result of this change of perspective was twofold. Firstly, some campaigners turned away from religion altogether; the Black Panthers, with their adherence to Marxism and Black Power, regarded Christianity as a tool of white oppression and religion more generally as the opium of the masses. Secondly, other campaigners turned towards the Muslim faith. Malcolm X joined the Nation of Islam (NOI) led by Elijah Mohammad. Similarly, Cassius Clay abandoned his name in favour of the

Islamic "Muhammad Ali", joined the NOI and then became one of the most fervent civil rights speechmakers of his generation. More debateable, however, is the connection between the growing popularity of Islam within the civil rights movement and the growing move towards violent revolution. On the one hand, Elijah Mohammad called the white man "the devil". On the other hand, Malcolm X ultimately left and then attacked the extremist position of the NOI, choosing instead to adopt a more moderate Sunni position which enabled him to secure something of a rapprochement with King – a reconciliation caught tragically short by Malcolm's assassination by NOI extremists in 1965. Moreover, Elijah Muhammad's youngest son Warith Muhammad took over leadership of Nation of Islam after his father's death and addressed Malcolm X's concerns by abolishing Elijah's racist teachings and explicitly recognizing American law.

In summary, the way in which the civil rights movement was radicalized was a move from nonviolent integration to violent separatism, which in turn had an impact on the social and religious complexion of the movement as well as its geographical focus. The main cause for this was the belief that the white power structure had been persuaded to pass legislation on Civil Rights, but that this only dealt with the symptoms and not the root causes of systemic racism in America: an issue which still causes severe tensions to this day, making King's words on the issue from 1967 as relevant now as they were then: "Let us be dissatisfied until that day when nobody will shout 'White Power!' - when nobody will shout 'Black Power!' ... the black man needs the white man and the white man needs the black man".

After swimming in Xiang River, Mao Zedong has a rest before a peasant's house (1958)

23. TO WHAT EXTENT DID MAO SUCCESSFULLY ACHIEVE AUTHORITARIAN RULE IN CHINA?

Mao's record as ruler of China is both complex and controversial. In 1980 the Chinese Communist Party (CCP) declared that he had been "70% right and 30% wrong" whilst the historian Immanuel Hsu prefers to argue that he was successful before 1957 and largely a failure thereafter. This complexity partly results from the fact that whilst some of his policies successfully resulted in Mao gaining an increasing degree of authoritarian control, the practical results of such policies stifled the development of Chinese society and its economy. This essay will argue that Mao was most securely in authoritarian control in the earlier part of his rule when he was able to demonstrate flexibility and pragmatism. As time wore on, his policies became more rigid; this helped him to play off different factions against each other, but it was at the expense of a genuinely broad base of popular support. By the end of his life, his position as an authoritarian leader was therefore ostensibly secure but fundamentally flawed.

In the first phase of his rule, roughly up to and including the First Five Year Plan (1953-1957), Mao instituted a series of policies which strengthened his authoritarian control despite being pragmatic in nature. Upon taking power, Mao immediately and cautiously declared through the Organic Law (1949) that his objective was to create a "democratic, peaceful, unified" China behind a "democratic dictatorship" of the "working class". Under the slogan "New Democracy", a new era of cooperation saw amnesties offered to government workers who agreed to support the new regime. Much more rigidly communist was the commitment to Lenin's "democratic centralism", which divided China into six administrative areas and then subdivided each to create a clear chain of command from the centre across the entire country. Executive power was wielded by the Central People's Government Council (CPGC), an elected body of 60 or so officials led by "Chairman" Mao, who exercised executive power alone when it was not in session. These arrangements were formalised in the 1954 Constitution.

Mao then proceeded to use his centralised authoritarian control to further impose his will upon his subordinates in the party and in the army. All military ranks were abolished and the Popular Liberation Army (PLA) became increasingly loyal to Mao personally. After seizing power, three separate PLA armies were sent to the outermost northern, western and southern provinces to forcibly bring them under control. By 1951 the process was complete. Gao and Rao, two of the heads of the six regions, were dismissed for building up a personal power base. Gao eventually committed suicide and Rao languished in prison. This sent out a clear message that nobody should consider their positions safe. By 1955, the number of people sent to labour camps was around 2 million; nine out of ten were political prisoners. The average number of prisoners held in the camps each year during Mao's time was 10 million; during his rule some 25 million people died in them.

Mao also used his growing authoritarian control to exert his will over religious minorities within China. Christian churches were closed and their property was confiscated during the Cultural Revolution of 1966–1976, when religion was attacked as one of the "Four Olds" ("old ideas, culture, customs and habits"). To give an appearance of tolerance, some churches were allowed to remain open as long as they "did not endanger the security of the state". These institutions were known as the "patriotic churches". The clergy had to accept the government's right to appoint priests and dictate doctrine, or risk being expelled from the country. China's religious policy led to a permanent rift with the Vatican; the Pope rejected the patriotic churches and refused to accept appointments made by the Chinese state.

Mao took a similarly hard line against Islam and Buddhism. With regard to Muslims, the PLA established military control in 1951 over Xinjiang, a distant western province with a large Muslim population bordering Soviet-controlled Mongolia. The CCP feared Xinjiang might fall into Soviet hands or even become part of a separatist movement, supported by neighbouring Muslim states. Tibetan Buddhists identified with the authority of their spiritual leader, the Dalai Lama. Around 60,000 Tibetans fought to defend their autonomy, but they did not have the weapons or the training to match the PLA, which took full control of Tibet within six months. In 1959, Tibet rose up against the Chinese occupation and the Chinese authorities reacted with brutality: an estimated 20% of the Tibetan population was arrested and half of them died in prison. The Dalai Lama fled to northern India and Tibetans were banned from even mentioning his name.

In economic terms, Mao's initial policies were characterised by initiatives designed to build up a broad base of popular support rather than focusing on an ideological obsession with securing his personal authoritarian control. He immediately took steps to restore the currency by slashing public spending, raising taxes and introducing a new currency, the Yuan. Inflation was thereby slashed from 1,000% in 1949 to only 15% in 1951. In the 1950 Agrarian Reform Law, Mao called for an end to "the land ownership system of feudal exploitation" and a redistribution of land and implements to landless peasants. Villagers held "struggle meetings" where they were encouraged to "speak bitterness" in show trials against landlords, who were in turn encouraged to offer "self-confessions" regarding their greed. Up to five million landlords are estimated to have been lynched. In the cities, entrepreneurs were allowed, initially, to retain ownership of their factories and then to share control by entering into "joint ownership" of businesses with the state. However, the "Three-Antis" and "Five-Antis" campaigns encouraged employees to inform on bosses. In Shanghai, an estimated 99% of businessmen were found guilty of at least one of the "Antis", more than 3,000 were arrested and an estimated 500 executions took place.

However, once again Mao very quickly moved away from generating popular enthusiasm for communism and moved instead towards democratic socialism, drawing power towards himself to secure further authoritarian control. The First Five Year Plan ended private peasant ownership and pursued collectivisation in an openly Stalinist manner, whilst factories were taken over by the state. Showcase projects were designed to demonstrate the new energy of the Chinese people. These included the Yangtze Bridge and the expansion of Tiananmen Square to 44 hectares in order to outdo Moscow's Red Square. Mao became known as the "emperor of the blue ants" in reference to the masses of workers who wore identical uniforms and marched under his banner.

Nevertheless, a key turning point which exposed the fragility of Mao's authoritarian control was the Hundred Flowers Campaign of 1956, which began with Mao ostensibly relaxing control and calling for a free exchange of ideas and criticism to stimulate further progress ("Let a Hundred Flowers bloom…let a hundred schools of thought contend"). Mao's motives remain unclear; he may have been feeling confident after the apparent success of the first Five-Year Plan, or perhaps was trying to trick his opponents into revealing themselves. Either way, the initiative was brought to a half after just a month characterised by a torrent of criticism, with Mao announcing the importance of distinguishing between "fragrant flowers" and "poisonous weeds". With the "poison" now exposed, Deng Xiaoping launched the Anti-Rightist Campaign, with millions more sent to labour camps. Although Mao depicted the whole episode as a cunning Machiavellian plot designed to lure his opponents into the open, it is equally possible that he was genuinely shocked by the degree and volume of criticism which resulted from the initial campaign and reacted out of panic and fear.

Further damage to Mao's authority resulted from the Great Leap Forward (1958-1961), which was economically disastrous and which fundamentally shook his reputation across the country and even within his own party. As early as 1955, Mao had complained that the CCP was "tottering along like a woman with bound feet, always complaining that others were going too fast". With this in mind, the Great Leap Forward merged the existing collectives (each containing an average of 300 families) into even larger units (containing up to 5000) which incorporated both agriculture and light industry. In their spare time, peasants were also expected to take part in the Anti-Pest Campaigns: sparrows were exterminated because they ate the grain before it was harvested, but this merely led to a proliferation of locusts which created even more damage (Mao eventually resorted to importing sparrows back into China from the USSR). Further agricultural failure resulted from adopting the pseudo-scientific methods of the Russian charlatan Trofim Lysenko, including his "deep ploughing" technique which led to an initial leap in production followed by a sudden collapse due to the exhaustion of the soil.

In terms of light industry, one of the most memorable failures of the Great Leap Forward was the building of "backyard furnaces" that would allow everyone to be part of the industrialization of China. These furnaces were built out of mud and straw, or whatever material was at hand, and, in a frenzy of enthusiasm, all manner of metal objects were collected for smelting (even, at the height of the campaign, essential farming implements). The end product was, predictably, of very poor quality. After criticisms of unrealistic targets in the 1958 Wuhan Conference, Mao reduced the steel and grain targets, but it was too little, too late. The result was the 1959-61 Great Famine which claimed the lives of up to 50 million people (and regarding which Mao commented "It is better to let half the people die so that the other half can eat their fill"). At the 1959 Lushan Conference, Peng Duhai attacked the famine resulting from the Great Leap Forward. He was fired as Minister of Defence and Mao announced that he would mobilise the people against the party if it did not fall in line (it did).

The degree to which Mao's authoritarian control had been shaken by the Hundred Flowers Campaign and the Great Leap Forward can be deduced from the fact that he retreated to what he referred to as the "Second Front" for several years after 1961, handing power and the initiative instead to the moderate reformers Liu Shaoqi and Deng Xiaoping. They reduced the size of the communes and allowed a revival of private markets so that farmers would be encouraged to sell their surplus stocks and to increase grain production. Although economically successful and broadly popular within the CCP, Mao did not approve; ideologically, he complained that the party was under threat from "capitalist roaders", and politically he became concerned that Liu would become "his Khrushchev, the servant who had denounced his master, Stalin". In a meeting with Mao, Liu had said that "history will judge you and me, and even cannibalism will go into the books". In 1965, the split between Mao and the party deepened when Yao Wenyuan, a theatre critic, claimed that a new play called *The Dismissal of Hai Rui from Office* was a thinly disguised allegory of Peng Dehuai's dismissal by Mao. Its author was Wu Han, Deputy Mayor of Beijing, who was promptly arrested and who died in jail in 1969.

It was at this time of declining power and authority that Mao decided to regain the initiative and re-establish his personal authoritarian control through what became known as the "Great Proletarian Cultural Revolution". In 1966, he was famously filmed swimming in the Yangtze river (traditionally regarded as the country's life force) to show to the world that he was still very much fit and in control. On 18 August 1966, a mass demonstration was then organized by Marshall Lin Biao in Tiananmen Square. Over a million people, mostly in their teens and twenties, waved their copies of Mao's *Little Red Book* of aphorisms and chanted slogans of worship, such as, "Mao Zedong is the red sun rising in the east!" and "Chairman Mao, may you live for a thousand years!". He then decided to use hardliners within the People's Liberation Army to counterbalance the growing power of his rivals within the CCP. General Lin Biao (already in charge of the PLA) was promoted to vice-chairman and placed at the head of the Campaign Against the Four Olds alongside Mao's wife, Jiang Qing (whom Mao called "the cultural purifier of the nation"). This heralded the true start of the Cultural Revolution, in which young bands of "Red Guards" engaged in a wave of wanton destruction under the slogans "to rebel is justified" and "bombard the headquarters". Millions rampaged across China, smashing temples, libraries and museums; children were urged to knock the heads off flowers to show their contempt for bourgeois concepts of beauty. Jiang Qing, a former actress, banned a whole range of "Western" activities including ballet, wrestling, poker and even the purchase of snacks.

In a social and economic sense, Immanuel Hsu argues that the Cultural Revolution was "anticultural, anti-intellectual and anti-scientific". The Red Guards became a "lost generation" whose education was interrupted and whose lives were blighted by long periods of exile. In 1981, in a rare moment of self-reflection, the CCP proclaimed it had "caused the most devastating setback and heavy losses to the party, the state and the people". Politically, however, Mao's position was strengthened considerably. He succeeded in purging the party of his moderate rivals: Liu Shoqui was sent to prison (where he died after being denied treatment for diabetes), Deng Xiaoping was sent to work in a factory, and his son was thrown out of a high window, suffering serious injuries that led to him being paralysed. By this stage, "like the emperors of the past, Mao was a patriarch, Helmsman, and even god-hero, who could do no wrong" (Hsu).

By this stage, Mao's cult of personality reached its zenith as he was proclaimed the "Great Teacher" and the "Great Helmsman". Perhaps the most bizarre aspect of this cult of hero-worship was the period of "Mango Fever". In 1968, an official delegation from Pakistan presented Mao with a consignment of forty mangoes. Unable to eat all these himself, Mao sent them to a group of "Revolutionary Workers" at a factory in Beijing. They were so moved by this gesture that they wrote a poem raising the fruit to the status of a holy relic ("Seeing that golden mango / Was as if seeing the Great Leader Chairman Mao!"). They then proceeded to send the mangoes on a diplomatic tour of China. One mango was even sent on a chartered flight to a Shanghai factory: upon arrival at the airport, it was driven solemnly through a procession of beating drums and people lining the streets until it reached its final destination. Millions of Chinese proceeded to purchase wax mangoes in glass cases to display as a reminder of Mao's munificence. One dentist in a small village, who had the audacity to compare a touring mango to a sweet potato was put on trial for malicious slander and executed.

The status of Mao's authoritarian control in China can therefore be seen as a series of clearly defined chronological chapters. The first period, up to and including the first Five Year Plan, was characterised by a degree of pragmatism which, whilst ostensibly based on "New Democracy" was fundamentally working towards a "democratic centralism" securing his authoritarian position. The second phase, which encompasses the Hundred Flowers Campaign and the Great Leap Forward, saw Mao superficially tightening his grip but against the background of growing dissent and socio-economic failure, causing him to retreat into the shadows for several years. The Great Proletarian Cultural Revolution, with good reason, is often regarded as Mao's high point of regaining authoritarian control, but even here his achievement was not without limits and failures. The 1971 rebellion of Lin Biao – Mao's anointed successor – demonstrated that the judgement of the "Great Helmsman" was fatally flawed. Mao's death in 1976 was not accompanied by the same sort of outpouring of grief as had characterised the passing of Premier Zhou Enlai earlier the same year. Mao's degree of authoritarian control was superficially impressive but fundamentally transient and inconsistent.

Mao meets Nixon, February 1972

24. HOW SUCCESSFUL WAS PRESIDENT NIXON'S FOREIGN POLICY?

Richard Nixon came to power in 1969 with the principal aim of bringing the Vietnam War to a swift conclusion. Nixon was determined to reduce the political and economic cost of America's longstanding commitment to 'containment' and 'rollback' of communism, which had led to disaster for Johnson in Vietnam and which had created dangerous tensions with China and the USSR. He quickly decided, with his National Security Advisor Henry Kissinger, that a policy of détente (de-escalation of tension) with the USSR and China would be the centrepiece of his strategy. This would not only place pressure on North Vietnam to negotiate, but would also disrupt Sino-Soviet relations and allow the USA to play each one off against the other – a policy he called "Triangular Diplomacy". By the time he was re-elected in a historic landslide in 1972, the Vietnam war was indeed almost over, and the legendary Cold Warrior had defied stereotypes by travelling to historic summits with China's Mao and the Soviet leader Brezhnev. However, the Vietnam War did not end victoriously or before he had escalated it into Laos and Cambodia. Moreover, by the time he was forced to step down in ignominy in 1974 following the Watergate

Scandal, he had also heavily involved the USA in both Chile and the Middle East in ways that remain deeply controversial and damaging.

Perhaps Nixon's greatest success came in February 1972 when he visited Chairman Mao in Beijing, setting in motion normalization of relations with the People's Republic of China. As a virulent and lifelong anti-communist, this was a bold and unexpected move from Nixon. Following the "Ping-Pong Diplomacy" of the American table-tennis team to China in 1971, Henry Kissinger, using the codename "Marco Polo", paid a secret visit to Beijing in July of that year and held extensive talks with Premier Zhou Enlai. In October, the UN withdrew Taiwan's right to take up China's seat in the United Nations Security Council and gave it instead to the People's Republic of China. Shortly afterwards Nixon commented that "We must remember the only time in history of the world that we have had any extended periods of peace is when there has been balance of power...I think it will be a safer world and better world if we have a strong, healthy United States, Europe, Soviet Union, China, Japan, each balancing the other, not playing one against the other". Nixon dubbed his visit to China "the week that changed the world", but notwithstanding his vision in this area, it has to be remembered that the visit was symbolic more than anything else and that he and Kissinger were really pushing at an open door, since the Chinese government was desperate for better relations with the USA due to its deteriorating relationship with the USSR. The Soviet Union had 25 divisions along the Chinese border and only 12 in Europe, and China had condemned Brezhnev for crushing the Prague Spring of 1968. Skirmishes in 1969 clearly highlighted that the Sino-Soviet split was ripe for exploitation.

The real value for the United States of Nixon's visit was the pressure that closer US-China relations placed upon the Soviet Union to follow suit. This policy paid dividends in May 1972, when Nixon became the first US President to visit Moscow. The SALT I treaty, signed by Nixon and Brezhnev at the end of the summit, froze the number of strategic ballistic missile launchers at existing levels, while the Anti-Ballistic Missile Treaty restricted both sides to only two sites for anti-ballistic missiles, with 200 missiles each. In a televised address from Moscow to the Soviet and American public, Nixon stated that "We have sought to...find ways of ensuring that future frictions between us would never embroiled our two nations, and therefore the world, in war". Further negotiations, following Brezhnev's visit to Washington in 1973 and Nixon's final visit to Moscow in 1974, extended arms control and disarmament measures and produced a Threshold Test Ban Treaty. These agreements have been seen as the central achievements of détente; the main criticism that can be levelled at Nixon in this regard was that he conducted much of the negotiations through the 'back channel' of Ambassador Dobrynin rather than through the State Department, and that the USSR secured a wheat deal from the USA on such favourable rates it was labelled by his opponents as the 'Great Grain Robbery'.

However, although on their own narrow terms the process of détente with the USSR and China can be seen as a success, it cannot be overlooked that the central purpose of this "triangular diplomacy" between the superpowers was to put pressure on the North Vietnamese to negotiate a settlement of the Vietnam War on terms advantageous to the United States. In this respect not only was the grand strategy of "triangulation" a signal failure, but so too was Nixon's attempt to "Vietnamise" the conflict. True, the Paris Peace Accords were signed under Nixon's administration (an achievement for which Kissinger controversially gained the Nobel Peace Prize) but within two years South Vietnam had fallen to the communists. Moreover, during the election campaign of 1968, we now know that in the "Chennault Affair" Nixon had deliberately used a backchannel to persuade South Vietnam to scupper President Johnson's proposed peace talks with the promise of a better deal once he was elected. Nixon's critics also point to the fact that he actually escalated the war still further by authorising attacks on the sovereign neutral territories of Laos and Cambodia starting in 1970; this secret mission was designated Operation Breakfast, after the morning Pentagon planning session at which it was devised between Kissinger and Nixon (the five missions and targets which followed were: Lunch, Snack, Dinner, Supper and Dessert. The entire series of missions was referred to – predictably - as Operation Menu). These were reckless acts of brinkmanship which could easily have escalated into a nuclear conflict with China or the Soviet Union, notwithstanding his simultaneous "shuttle diplomacy" with Brezhnev and Mao.

Nevertheless, in reality it was in the Middle East, not Vietnam, where the international situation threatened most closely to escalate into another World War. In this area, it is clear that US foreign policy saved Israel, but was economically disastrous; but to suggest that Nixon was personally responsible for it stretches the facts of the case. In point of fact, Nixon was on the verge of a nervous breakdown, mired in the Watergate Scandal, when Egyptian and Syrian armies launched a devastating surprise attack upon the Israelis in occupied parts of Egypt and Syria in the October War of 1973. As a result, policy decisions were largely left in the hands of Henry Kissinger, who took the decision to withhold arms from the Israelis in an attempt to force them to the negotiating table. Nixon did decisively stepped in at the last moment to "save Israel" by providing weapons in Operation Nickel Grass, but it was Kissinger's initial game of brinkmanship which paid dividends:

as anticipated, Israel was shaken out of the complacency she had wallowed in since her victory in the 1967 Six-Day War, and ultimately returned the Sinai to Egypt and welcomed Sadat to speak at the Knesset in 1977 (the first step towards the Camp David Accords of 1979). More negatively, US policy provoked an angry reaction from King Faisal of Saudi Arabia, and when Congress nevertheless proceeded to approve a $2.2 billion budget to help Israel, OPEC imposed an oil embargo on the West. Oil prices in the USA quadrupled, and this "Oil Shock" ended the long boom of economic growth that had existed since the 1950s. As Stephen Ambrose puts it, "there is no doubt that Nixon… made it possible for Israel to win, at some risk to his own reputation and at great risk to the American economy. He knew that his enemies…would never give him credit for saving Israel. He did it anyway".

Moving away from the Middle East, a consideration of US policy in Chile leads to the damning verdict that Nixon's policy was successful in its objectives, but that these objectives were morally reprehensible. Infamously, Nixon was determined to secure the overthrow of the democratically elected Salvador Allende, whose nationalisation of American business interests such as the telecommunications company Chitelco had infuriated the President (much as Castro's nationalisation of the United Fruit company in Cuba had incensed Eisenhower more than a decade earlier). Although it is tempting to do so for purposes of the narrative, it would be a mistake to idealise Allende; in 1972, the Cuban Packages Scandal rocked his government when it became clear that his "League of Personal Friends" had been provided with several thousand AK47s by Fidel Castro; this had led to the Chamber of Deputies passing the CODE Resolution accusing him of undermining the constitution. Nevertheless, Nixon's policy towards the Allende regime was utterly brutal. In a notorious meeting with CIA chief

Richard Helms he decided to cut off aid to Chile in order to "make the economy scream" and to make contact with opposition groups in order to provide them with the necessary funding – millions of dollars were put at the disposal of the CIA – to undermine Allende in any way possible. Kissinger justified this saying that America could not "stand by and watch a country go communist due to the irresponsibility of its own people". Although in his defence there is no evidence that Nixon or the CIA were directly connected to the Pinochet coup which ended in the death of Allende in 1973, it cannot be denied that they did their utmost to create the conditions which precipitated the coup, thereby condemning Chile to almost 20 years of brutal military dictatorship.

To conclude, Nixon is a President responsible for some towering achievements: the boldness of his policy with regard to the USSR and China, especially in the Cold War tensions of the time, is worthy of genuine credit. Nevertheless, US achievements in the Middle East were offset by the economic damage they precipitated and were as much the work of Kissinger than of Nixon. Similarly, his actions in Chile, whilst achieving his objectives, were based on a policy which was morally repugnant. In this sense, considering the successes and failures of Nixon's foreign policies depends largely on how one chooses to measure success, and how narrowly one decides to focus on Nixon the man rather than the Nixon administration.

General Pinochet pictured in Santiago, 1989

25. WHAT WAS THE POLITICAL AND ECONOMIC IMPACT OF MILITARY RULE IN CHILE BETWEEN 1973 AND 1989?

Following the overthrow of President Allende in Chile by General Pinochet on September 11th 1973, the impact of military rule was profound. Politically, the regime legitimised dictatorship and carried out a brutal campaign of repression and censorship. This in turn exacerbated severe economic dislocation and social distress, not least due to the withdrawal of aid from foreign powers; Pinochet's response was to pursue radical economic policies, which in turn created further political opposition. Nevertheless, although an authoritarian ruler, Pinochet was not a totalitarian one. By the late 1980s the Chilean economy had been liberalised, and in 1988 he was removed from office after a democratic referendum and without further bloodshed.

The immediate political impact of military rule upon Chile was characterised by dictatorship, brutal repression and censorship on a scale not seen since the heyday of Fascism in 1930s Europe. Immediately upon coming to power, Pinochet suspended the 1925 democratic constitution in favour of a rotating presidency held by military generals; within weeks even this was jettisoned in favour of a one-man dictatorship. By the end of the year he openly stated that there was no set timetable for a return to civilian rule. A constitutional referendum was held in Chile on 11 September 1980, approved by over two-thirds of voters, which ensured that Pinochet could remain as President of the Republic for a further eight years with increased powers, after which he would face a re-election referendum. This move towards dictatorship was accompanied by brutal repression of Chilean dissidents in the military, politics and culture. Combined with "Operation Cleanliness", a thoroughgoing programme of book-burning and censorship, these actions led sociologist Soledad Bianchi (who went into exile in France during the military dictatorship era) to claim that Chile experienced a "cultural blackout" during the Pinochet years.

The most notorious symbol of Pinochet's brutality was the "Caravan of Death", the murderous squads who rounded up thousands of opponents in the national football stadium in the days following the coup with the announcement: "Attention, human sewage pipes. Human squalor. You are war prisoners. And you may all die here". This was the fate of Victor Jara, iconic protest singer, who was arrested the day after the Pinochet coup, interned in the stadium, and then forced to play guitar after having his hands smashed by rifle butts before finally being executed and dumped outside the entrance as a grim warning to other prisoners being brought inside. Other notable victims were high-ranking military figures, many of whom were hunted down and executed on foreign soil as part of "Operation Condor". Most infamous was the state-sponsored assassination of Orlando Letelier, Defence Minister to Allende. He fled to Washington DC and lobbied against Pinochet's government ("They were born traitors and they will be known forever as fascist traitors"). In 1976 he was killed by a car bomb in Washington DC – the first act of state-sponsored terrorism ever committed on US soil.

Later in the 1970s, the regime's state police, the *DINA*, began to use a tactic of *Falsos Enfrentamientos* (fake combats). This meant that dissidents who were murdered by the DINA had their deaths reported in the media as if they had occurred in a mutual gunfire exchange. The Rettig Report (1991) determined that 2,279 persons were killed for political reasons in this manner. This figure included 957 "disappeared" after arrest and 164 "victims of political violence", many tortured in places like the notorious *Colonia Dignidad*. According to Peter Kornbluh, "routine sadism was taken to extremes". Prisoners were immersed in vats of urine and excrement, and one technique known as "the telephone" involved the torturer slamming "his open hands hard and rhythmically against the ears of the victim" until they were rendered deaf. Another technique was to play a "Torture Tape" of pop music (including, rather bizarrely, the serene "My Sweet Lord" by former Beatle George Harrison) on a permanent loop at full volume.

In economic terms, the military coup and its radical reversal of Allende's left-wing policies of nationalisation and heavy public spending initially created dislocation and chaos. The economic crash which came in 1975 led not to the moderation of Pinochet's policies, but rather their further radicalisation. He put the economy in the hands of a group of Chilean economists known as "The Chicago Boys", trained in orthodox free-market economics by Milton Friedman ("Gradualism is not feasible"). Appointing Sergio de Castro as finance minister, Pinochet gave the Chicago Boys free reign to implement their economic manifesto ("The Brick") which saw public spending slashed by 25% in just six months in a process which Friedman referred to as "Shock Treatment". Social services predictably suffered from chronic underfunding. In health, private health insurance plans (FONASA) replaced state provision, exacerbating unequal access to healthcare between rich and poor. In education, the government devolved school investment to the localities, providing state subsidies to private schools depending on the number of students they managed to attract and charge. The result of this was that the poorest 44% of young people did not complete secondary school compared to more than 70% under Allende. Compounding the problem was Pinochet's chronic human rights record, which led to the US cutting aid to Chile in 1976 ("Why should we squander money on tyrants, giving them the weapons to hold down their own people?", asked Senator Alan Cranston). Great Britain, which had supplied the bulk of the Chilean navy, followed suit with trade sanctions in 1980, and the French in 1981. This was met by Pinochet with "a blend of resentment and anxiety", in the words of the US Ambassador to Santiago.

More positively, however, another crisis in the mid-1980s finally saw Pinochet move towards a more moderate economic position characterised by the promotion of a mixed economy. Privatisation and free market enterprise remained a central tenet of his thinking, but he also appointed a new finance minister, Hernan Buchi, who renationalised the Chilean copper industry (CODELCO) which was responsible for 85% of Chilean exports. From 1985 the economy grew at robust rates, fuelled by strong capital flows from abroad, aggressive export promotion, a well-managed fiscal system and investments in infrastructure which sharply reduced unemployment. As the then finance minister, Alejandro Foxley, said in a 1991 interview: "We may not like the government that came before us. But they did many things right. We have inherited an economy that is an asset."

Despite the evidence that the political impact of Pinochet's rule was barbaric, his economic policies demonstrate that his regime was never totalitarian. Resistance was never crushed, as demonstrated for example by the brightly coloured patchwork pictures (*arpilleras*) made by women in Chile, depicting scenes of hardship and violence. These women were organized by the Vicariate of Solidarity, a pro-democracy group run by the archbishop of Santiago. The Vicariate was responsible for finding a place to meet, providing supplies and buying the finished *arpilleras* and selling them abroad. As a result of such examples of continued resistance, when Pinochet held a fresh referendum in 1988 to confirm his position, he was roundly defeated in the polls. Following his defeat, Pinochet and opposition forces agreed to revise the 1980 Constitution. The 54 proposed amendments were approved by 91% of voters in a referendum on 30 July 1989. Presidential and parliamentary elections took place as scheduled on 14 December 1989. The opposition candidate - Patricio Aylwin of the Christian Democrats - won the election with 55% of the vote and took office on 11 March 1990. The newly elected Congress was sworn in that same day and the rule of Pinochet was officially over.

In conclusion, the negative impact of military rule in Chile can hardly be overstated. For the bulk of his rule, economic libertarianism existed in a completely unsustainable dichotomy with political repression. In his favour, Pinochet's was, in the end, finally able to see the error of the unbridled capitalism promoted by the "Chicago Boys" and the political untenability of staying in power after his failure in the 1988 referendum. Nevertheless, this is overshadowed by his human rights abuses as dictator of Chile. Therefore, whilst his death in 2008 meant that he was able to avoid facing trial for his crimes, he is unlikely to be acquitted in the court of history.

ABOUT THE AUTHOR

Russel Tarr has a degree in Modern World History from Lady Margaret Hall, Oxford University and a History teaching qualification from Birmingham University. He has been a full-time teacher of History and Politics since 1997 and is currently Head of History at the International School of Toulouse in France.

His previously published works include *Luther and the Reformation in Europe 1500-64* and the two volumes of *A History Teaching Toolbox*. He also writes regularly for the international press and delivers freelance training courses to history teachers.

Russel is also author of www.activehistory.co.uk, which provides innovative teaching resources, worksheets and online simulations for the history classroom, and www.classtools.net, which freely provides online game generators and learning templates.

Russel can be contacted at russeltarr@activehistory.co.uk.

Made in the USA
Middletown, DE
09 September 2020